Meeting Managers' Information Needs

Helen Butcher

A Managing Information Report

Series Editor: Moira Duncan

Published by
Aslib, The Association for Information Management.
Staple Hall, Stone House Court, London EC3A 7PB

Tel: +44 (0) 171 903 0000
Fax: +44 (0) 171 903 0011
Email: *pubs@aslib.co.uk*
WWW: *http://www.aslib.co.uk/*

© Helen Butcher, 1998

ISBN 0 85142 405 8

Aslib, The Association for Information Management, is a world class corporate membership organisation with over 2000 members in some 70 countries. Aslib actively promotes best practice in the management of information resources. It lobbies on all aspects of the management of and legislation concerning information at local, national and international levels.

Aslib provides consultancy and information services, professional development training, conferences, specialist recruitment, Internet products, and publishes primary and secondary journals, conference proceedings, directories and monographs.

Contents

Chapter 3 –
Why do managers need information?   45

Introduction

In recent years there has been a huge increase in the amount of information available to both businesses and the wider society. This increase has largely been the result of an improvement in the information and communication technologies which have revolutionised the collection, storage, organisation and delivery of information as well as providing new tools with which the information can be manipulated. For many organisations these changes have been so great that the problem of finding information to satisfy their business needs has been largely replaced by the problem of coping with too much information. Similarly, the focus of much discussion among information professionals and those working in information systems has turned from that of the provision of information to the organisation to the problem of managing the information within the organisation.

There is also an increasing recognition of the importance of information and its management among writers. As Drucker (1995) points out, 'the corporation that is now emerging is being designed around a skeleton: information, both the corporation's new integrating system and its articulation.'

Information is used in decision-making at all levels and within all functions in the organisation. Information about the organisation's internal processes and functions is required to ensure that its goals and targets will be met. Information is required as part of the strategic planning process and there is an ongoing need for information of the sort that will trigger entrepreneurial activity. Yet the information by itself will not guarantee the success of the enterprise, other factors must also be present:

- Information which is of potential use to the individual must be recognised as such. This implies that the individual has some knowledge of the decisions which he/she will be required to take either now or at some future date; he/she must also have some understanding of the information which is required to facilitate those decisions. To be aware of at least some of one's own information needs is relatively common but a successful enterprise requires that its employees are aware of the information needs of others within the organisation also. This can be very difficult to achieve, particularly in functionally differentiated organisations.
- To be regarded as useful, most types of information must be processed in some way:

- if the information is likely to be useful to others in the organisation then the processing of the information may involve merely passing the information to a colleague in a conversation, emailing to staff, or alerting people to it in a report or presentation. Alternatively, it may involve ensuring that the information is stored in the corporate computerised information system to be retrieved at a later date by any interested party. There are other many ways in which information may be processed for use by others.

- information which is to be used in one's own tasks and decision-making activity may be processed in several ways, a few examples of which are given below:

  - the information may be acted upon immediately; decisions may be made or decisions already made may be changed,

  - the information may trigger action of some kind – for instance, where information is received that a supply of a vital raw material may be restricted then this may trigger the action of locating another source,

  - the information may be filed with other information on the same or similar topics; such filing may be manual or automated,

  - the information may be internalised and so become part of the manager's internal model or perception of how the world is. Such information may influence the manner in which he/she makes later decisions.

It is now clear, however, that it is the *human* processing of the information, rather than the mere collection and storage of information in computerised information systems, which will determine the success or otherwise of the enterprise. Many organisations are recognising the value added by human information processing and the improvement in the knowledge-base of the organisation which results. This has led to a desire to foster knowledge creation by investing in the human intellectual capital store of the organisation and by ensuring that the knowledge of individuals is leveraged within the organisation.

So, as the emphasis in many organisations moves from the *mediation* of the information (the technology) and towards the *use* of the information, this book attempts to provide the reader with an understanding of some of those factors which underlie the use of information and the creation of knowledge by individuals and within the organisation as a whole. Chapter 1 considers how information flows around the organisation, and between the organisation and the external environment. Factors such as lack of communication and inappropriate corporate systems are acknowledged to act as barriers to the free flow of information but chapter 1 also considers how the systematic distortion of information and organisational politics may severely hinder attempts to improve the flow of information.

New technologies such as videoconferencing, datawarehousing, electronic data interchange (EDI), document-management systems, intranets and groupware are now in use in many organisations and chapter 1 discusses their impact on the organisation's information-handling capability. Consideration is also given to the creation of a learning organisation using these new technologies and the new structures created often as a result of business process re-engineering.

Chapter 2 focuses more specifically on the manager rather than the organisation. Several writers have pointed out that managers are required to make decisions about both the day-to-day running of the organisations and also its future strategy and they point out that information is vital for such decisions. Yet managers frequently fail to make use of the information provided by formally constituted information providers within the organisation such as the library, information unit, strategic business unit and research unit. Similarly, in many organisations there are complaints that the automated corporate information systems do not provide the information which the manager requires, and that the information which is provided is rarely in an appropriate format. There is clearly some discrepancy between the information which the manager needs and that which those charged with the provision of information perceive that the manager needs. In attempting to explain the nature of managerial work and the skills and knowledge which the manager requires to perform the differing tasks, chapter 2 attempts to explain some of the reasons for the problems outlined above.

Chapter 3 looks in a little more detail at the tasks for which a manager requires information. It discusses the types of decisions a manager is required to make and the types of information which will be required for each type of decision. It also considers the methodologies available to determine managerial information needs and discusses why managers may have problems with using information in decision-making. Chapter 3 also discusses whether there is evidence that information actually improves managerial performance.

Much has been written about the information which is available for business, yet, as indicated above, information professionals often complain that managers fail to make use of these business sources. It is clear that at least some information is required in order to make decisions; it is also equally clear that many managers seem to make decisions without recourse to those information sources which the information professional would regard as vital. Chapter 4 tries to identify the sources which the manager *actually* uses as opposed to those which many in the information profession believe he/she should use. It discusses why the manager seems to show a marked preference for verbal media while often shunning written reports. This theme is continued in chapter 5 which considers the characteristics which information should possess to improve the likelihood that it will be considered to be potentially useful by managers. Much has been written about the characteristics of 'good' information. It has been suggested that such characteristics will include timeliness, relevance, appropriateness and comprehensiveness, yet if ,as reported, so many managers complain about information overload perhaps we need to question whether all these characteristics are still valid. If, as shown in chapter 3, managers do not want, and indeed cannot use, vast quantities of information then it may be that 'comprehensive' information provision is not only unnecessary but possibly even harmful to the decision-making process in some circumstances.

The book concludes with a consideration of some of the implications of the findings provided in the text together with some thoughts about how managerial information needs might be best catered for in the future.

BIBLIOGRAPHY

Drucker, Peter. 'The Information Executives Truly Need.' *Harvard Business Review,* January/February 1995, pp. 54-62.

Chapter 1

The organisation, the environment and information

INTRODUCTION

Some organisations are set up for a specific purpose, others simply evolve; however, all organisations have aims and objectives which are either stated or implicit. Over time, organisations also develop a culture and norms; systems and processes evolve, together with a specific method of 'doing things'. These traditions must be respected by those who work in them and by those who have dealings with them, such as their suppliers and customers, and they are frequently reflected in the organisational structure which usually evolves as the company grows. In the past, organisations have often chosen a functional differentiation into departments such as finance, marketing, personnel and sales, thus recognising a perceived need for specialists in these areas who bring different experience, skills and knowledge to the organisation. More recently, however, some organisations have chosen a flatter hierarchical structure with few layers of management and a less functional differentiation. Whatever the structure, however, information must flow between people within the organisation, and between the organisation and the external world. Such communication is vital for the successful functioning of the organisation, and most organisations establish formal mechanisms and processes with vertical and horizontal channels of communication to provide for the exchange of such information. In all organisations, systems and procedures must be devised to encourage people to communicate information and cooperate in the sharing of information within the organisation and between the organisation and the external world.

Within the organisation such communication mechanisms may take the form of regular meetings between managers and staff within functions (where they exist) and interdepartmental meetings between managers of different functions. There are likely to be formal minutes of many such meetings, monthly reports of activities may be circulated, and memos and phone calls exchanged where appropriate. The organisation may also set up integrating activities such as cross-functional teams to facilitate the free and easy exchange of information. Different functions often have differing time scales, targets and priorities and the amount of information that is needed to maintain the interdependence of departments will depend on their level of integration. In organisations where team-working is emphasised and where there is a flat hierarchical structure, the functions are likely to be less fragmented and better integrated, and there is likely to be a better flow of information as a result. Consequently, there will be less of a requirement for formal mechanisms to facilitate information sharing. However, in organisations where there is a high degree of functional independence it is likely there will be a need for more face-to-face interactions to enable those from the different functions to develop a shared understanding. This is particularly important in highly specialised functions such as law and finance which rely on a technical short-hand which may be impenetrable to the layman. As shared interpretations develop, however, it is likely that the staff will be able to communicate satisfactorily using phone calls, electronic mail (if available) and memos rather than face-to-face meetings.

THE ORGANISATION AND ITS ENVIRONMENT

There is also an interaction between the organisation and the outside world; few organisations can exist independently of their environment. The relationship between the organisation and the wider environment may be very complex, particularly if the organisation has a global presence. The organisation will need to interact with many groups of stakeholders such as customers, suppliers, distributors; advisers such as bankers, accountants, consultants and often lobby and consumer groups. The organisation develops policies to deal with these stakeholder relationships; for instance, there may be a policy of satisfying the customer by providing good quality at a competitive price. There may be a policy of offering suppliers access to the organisation's inventory information to enable a speedier, more cost-effective and efficient restocking and thus largely eliminate costly warehousing.

In addition to offering opportunities for business, however, the external world also imposes constraints on what the organisation may do. Suppliers and distributors, for instance, may impose operational constraints – the organisation might require that parts and raw materials should be delivered within 24 hours while the suppliers and distributors might be unable to comply with this timescale. The organisation must comply with the law and so is constrained by the rules governing many aspects of its operations such as employment, health and safety, export and finance. Stakeholders also impose constraints; for instance, trade unions may refuse to allow the organisation to do certain things considered prejudicial to its members; shareholders' requirements may include the provision of a regular dividend, thus constraining the amount of money available for investment. Organisations also often find that it is prudent to take account of public interest and the views of lobby groups, economic and political groups, environmental and consumer groups, local and public authorities, statutory bodies, and industrial lobbies. Any organisation which is deemed to be acting in a manner prejudicial to the public good might find that their public relations and even their market share are seriously damaged. For instance, in 1995, when Shell announced its intention to sink a redundant oil drilling platform, there was enormous public opposition and a boycott of its products in some countries. As a consequence the company was obliged to abandon the idea.

Competitive pressures will also constrain what the organisation can do. Each organisation must compete for staff and resources in addition to market share. The organisation will also be constrained because of its need to cooperate with other organisations such as banks, advertising agencies, lawyers, even sometimes erstwhile competitors.

Constraints on the organisation will cause it to alter its behaviour or limit its actions and its decision-making will inevitably reflect the trade-off between the desired ends and the constraints. Some decisions may even be taken as a direct result of consultation with others such as staff, interest groups and other stakeholders. This consultation is aimed, in part at least, to generate understanding and gain acceptance for the particular course of action.

Clearly, the more diverse and complex the organisation and the more dynamic the organisation's environment then the more complicated will be the interaction between them. Figure 1 demonstrates some of these interactions and also the complexity of the flows of information within the organisation and between it and the external world since increases in the complexity of the environment usually increase the demand for information.

THE FLOW OF INFORMATION IN ORGANISATIONS

As many organisations begin to recognise the value of their information and intellectual capital and have taken measures to improve its quality, collection and processing, management attention is now focusing on the flow of the information around the organisation in an attempt to leverage learning and knowledge.

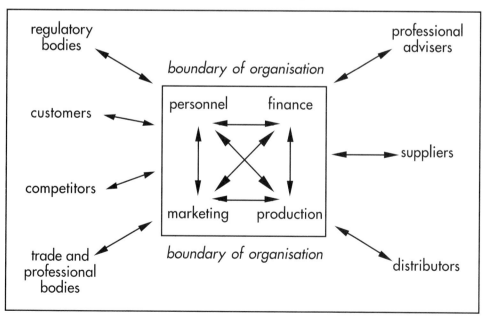

Figure 1 – The flow of information within the organisation and between it and the external environment.

For instance, in 1994 in a survey commissioned by Reuters, Taylor and Nelson reported that 88% of managers said that the free flow of information was vital to their business. The same survey, however, revealed that in many organisations there are barriers which impede the free flow of information – 67% of the managers surveyed reported that information did not flow freely within their organisations; the reasons for this merit consideration.

Barriers to the free flow of information in the organisation

Several factors influence the ease with which information flows around an organisation. Many of these factors – such as organisational politics, lack of coordination of organisational effort, communication barriers, distortion of information and inappropriate organisational systems – may also cause problems for the organisation in other areas of its operations.

Organisational politics

Information is often used as an instrument of power in organisations, but it is not merely the withholding of information which causes problems for both the manager and the organisation as a whole. Information may be perceived as a threat to existing power bases of individuals and groups within the organisation. Thus, existing organisational attitudes and managerial approaches will determine what information is collected and how it is processed and disseminated because the dominant personalities (for instance, senior managers) are likely to frame issues in ways which will preserve their own power bases. Such managers may prefer ambiguous information which can be interpreted in self-enhancing or equivocal ways, or in a manner which furthers their own self interest. This may cause serious problems for the organisation, particularly when strategic issues being decided because such issues require a broad sweep of thinking, even requiring those involved to question the most fundamental tenets of the organisation and its place in the environment. A lack of appropriate information at this time may compromise the decision-making process within the organisation, thus threatening its future.

The Reuters survey (1994) revealed how widespread the effect of organisational politics is when 67% of managers stated that they believe that information does not flow freely in their organisations for political reasons; this percentage rose to 71% among middle managers. The managers complained that information was hoarded so it could be announced at moments to the advantage of the senior manager; one manager in the survey even said, '... internal politics impedes the flow of information in this company. It is always in someone's interest not to tell someone else'.

This information politicking was reported to have several effects:

- managers were embarrassed and frustrated at their lack of what they perceived to be vital information;

- time was wasted searching for information which was already available to others;
- sales and business opportunities were lost;
- decision-making and planning were made more difficult because potentially useful information was not available;
- business did not run as smoothly as it would have done had the information been freely available.

While many of the problems of organisational politics seem to be caused by senior managers, middle managers who collect data also may also inhibit the free flow of information around the organisation. It is often against their own interests to change data collection methods and processing, even when instructed to do so by those responsible for decision-making. Such a change may cause disruption to their routines and require new working methods and extra work, so they may continue with the old data collection and processing methods which are often based on ease of collection rather than the needs of the organisation.

Information distortion
Much of the information collected and processed by the organisation is distorted, and this may impede the free-flow of information around the organisation. Such distortion may not be deliberate, it may be caused by the viewpoint or bias of the information source – *The Guardian* or *The Financial Times,* for instance, often provide differing perspectives on the same event. However, in many organisations the distortion of the information is more insidious. Much information is collected for some specific purpose or with someone's agenda in mind and this agenda may not be apparent to other members of the organisation. Such information may be collected by individuals within a climate of conflict or self-interest, or as back-up for a decision which they have already made. It may also be collected to prove a point or demonstrate more knowledge than a peer – few people can provide information without it being clouded by their own agenda, whatever that might be.

This distortion by those who are both collecting and providing information may cause serious problems for the organisation as it may make the identification of current and potential problems very difficult. The organisation may believe it has collected and acted upon quality information, not realising how badly the information has been distorted and the damage that may be caused to the organisation as a result. Several types of information distortion have been reported in organisations:

- Good news syndrome – good news usually circulates quickly while bad news may be blocked. There seems to be a natural tendency in organisations to suppress or alter bad news; in the worse cases unfavourable information may be ignored or regarded as at variance with other information already available and so unreliable. This is understandable – we all like to create a good impression and are keen that our strengths should be recognised, while we seek to downplay information which is unfavourable to our point of view. This tendency to distort and even block bad news, however, can cause considerable problems for the organisation. It may cause senior managers to have an unrealistic view of the business environment and mean that they are not alerted to current and potential problems until it may be too late to do anything about them; critical decisions may be taken based on inaccurate or misleading information.

- Exaggeration – in some organisations, particularly those with traditional structures and a functional differentiation, managers may feel that they are in competition with each other for finite resources. In such an environment managers may exaggerate the positive benefits of their own projects or functions to secure funding, while attempting to minimise the benefits of projects of those with whom they feel they are in competition. Managers are aware that resources tend to be allocated to those who produce favourable information rather then those who produce bad news. Where such a project is of material or strategic importance to the organisation, however, this might considerably distort the organisation's view of itself and of its future prospects. Consider, for example, when a significant new product is market-tested; if initial results are less then successful then this fact might be down-played lest the project be stopped. The result may be that those planning the future sales of the organisation might expect a considerable contribution to profitability to be made by this product and make decisions based on this assumption with potentially disastrous results for the organisation.

- Groupthink – the problem of distorted information may be further exacerbated by 'groupthink', a word coined to describe the phenomenon where groups of people who are called upon to make decisions withhold any objections they may have because they do not wish to be seen as at variance with the rest of group as this might endanger group harmony and might result in personal recrimination. Groupthink is reputed to have been responsible for the fiasco of the Bay of Pigs invasion during the Kennedy administration – several members of President Kennedy's cabinet admitted after the event that they had had considerable reservations about the invasion but did not wish to seem out of step with others and so did not voice them.

Many people are aware that information is rarely innocent and consequently make allowances for distortion of information. They realise that most individuals report information with a bias that reflects self-interest or their own particular vantage point and so they make allowances for this. But communication in organisations is very complicated and it may not always be obvious what an individual's vantage point is. In such circumstances it might be difficult to make allowances for the 'she would say that, wouldn't she' phenomenon, particularly when such information is associated with non-routine and/or strategic considerations.

Larson and King (1992) report that the tendency to distort information has effects wider than problems in decision-making. Those providing the bad news may suffer even if the information is true. The bearers of bad tidings may be regarded as troublemakers and be isolated in the organisation or even worse. Larson and King (1992) report the case of the American Eagle pilot who reported that the plane might not be safe in icy conditions. He was fired one week before the plane crashed in just the conditions about which he expressed concern.

This distortion of information can be counteracted; ways can be found to ensure that the information which the organisation receives is less distorted. In many organisations there is a flattening of managerial hierarchies, which in itself tends to reduce distortion because such flattening is often accompanied by greater decentralisation of decision-making and consequently less information needs to be sent upwards so there is less scope for distortion. Similarly, where decisions are made closer to the action, there is less incentive to distort the information.

There may still be some situations, however, in which subordinates feel threatened by managerial reaction to poor results. Information is often distorted because subordinates fear the consequences of their reports of bad news. This fear can be eliminated to some extent by making it clear that there will be no censure attached to those reporting bad news; rather, such news will be acted on as a way of improving performance. Indeed, in some organisations, employees are actively encouraged to seek out problems and put them right. Such an approach requires a redefinition of what constitutes 'favourable' information in the organisation but it may substantially improve the quality of the information which circulates within the organisation by removing the perceived consequences of its reporting.

Larson and King (1992) suggest that distortion of information may also be alleviated to some extent by employing external people to audit new proposals or cost new projects. In principle such consultants should provide an objective view of the situation and provide 'agenda free' information. However, Larson and King (1992) point out that there is some research to suggest that even consultants are sometimes reluctant to go against the view which the organisation expects as they too may suffer the consequences of reporting 'bad' news and hence may not get repeat business.

Lack of coordination of effort

The size and complexity of many organisations frequently results in a lack of coordination of effort of its information collection procedures. As a result, while many departments in the organisation may have a clear idea of the nature of their own particular external environment because they have appropriate information collection and processing mechanisms in place, the organisation as a whole may be missing the total picture. This lack of coordination of effort seriously restricts the flow of information around the organisation and may also seriously affect its strategic aspirations. The problem is caused partly by organisational design: functional organisations tend to be highly differentiated and it may be difficult to coordinate effort across them. Aguilar (1967) suggests that this causes three problems:

- duplication of effort in the information collection and storage process;

- missed opportunities because of failure to make use of information available within the organisation;

- failure of individuals and functions to collect information which might be of use to others.

This lack of coordination of effort may be very expensive in terms of both time and money, and it would seem there is much to be gained by coordinating information scanning, collecting and storing activities across the organisation. Aguilar (1967) suggests that there are several ways in which coordination of information activities might be improved:

- To begin with, an organisation should consider an information mapping exercise to determine precisely the extent of its current information holdings, the locations of these holdings and how and when such information is updated. Many departments within organisations build their own applications and collect information specifically for their own needs with little or no thought for the needs of the organisation as a whole. Such departmental resources can be a valuable source of information for the other functions as well as the organisation as a whole.

- Management should encourage an awareness of the information needs of other departments and individuals. This may not be easy to achieve – though inter-departmental meetings, cross-functional task forces and staff coordinators may help. Some companies have tried to encourage coordination of effort and improvement in the flow of information around the organisation by insisting on the reporting of all external meetings and copious use of reports and memoranda to ensure that everyone has access to all information. This 'solution', however, may cause more problems than it solves as there is a chance that this will result in too much information, thus reducing the likelihood that relevant and important information will be identified.

- Strategic planning – most organisations have strategic plans, and the strategic planning process should facilitate the collection of information and increase awareness of the importance of collecting information about the external environment as it will define those issues which are critical to the success of the plan and hence of the organisation. The strategic planning process should increase the general awareness of organisational activities and encourage interdepartmental communication and the flow of information.

Inappropriateness of organisational systems

The flow of information in an organisation may be further hampered by the inappropriateness of some of its systems. These may include any formal information collection facilities such as the library or information unit as well as its automated information systems.

A recognition of the importance of information to the organisation together with the availability of new information and communication technologies has resulted in the processing of much more information from both internal and external sources. The systems used for this information processing, however, are often inappropriate for the needs of the organisation and may be very expensive.

Information collection and research facilities
Organisations often respond to the perceived need for information about the external environment by the creation of formal units for monitoring and analysing the external environment. Such units may be called libraries, Research Departments, Strategic Business Units, Information Units, Business Analysis Units or Environmental Scanning Departments. The remit of such units varies; an Information Unit may be charged with the task of responding to queries and researching problems posed by members of the organisation while the members of a Strategic Business Unit may expected to determine the strategic problems of the organisation and suggest solutions – a more proactive role. For many organisations, however, the creation of such units has often proved largely ineffective. The units are often staffed with highly qualified and capable staff and usually equipped with state-of-the-art information systems, but in many organisations these units are perceived as marginal to the main activities of the organisation. The problem seems to be that many organisations create such units without any understanding of the dynamics of information use within the organisation and among its individual members. The assumption seems to be that the organisation needs information and therefore the creation of a formal mechanism to provide information will provide information which the organisation and its individual members can and will use. This has proved to be a very expensive and false assumption in many organisations. Many organisations now believe successful information collection and processing requires that the whole organisation becomes sensitive to the information needs of its members; it is not a function that can be easily delegated to a formally constituted department.

Several reports from writers such as Ghosal and Kim (1986), McGee and Prusak (1992) and Reuters (1994) have commented on the failure of information units and similar formally constituted units to cater for the information needs of organisations and their members:

- The information they collect is largely context independent – it is stored on the assumption that such information will prove useful in the future, this may or may not be the case.

- The creation of such units is often based on a misunderstanding of how decisions are made in organisations:
    - Much of the information is collected with little regard for the decisions which need to be made within the organisation. Indeed, most organisations systematically collect more information than they need, yet at the same time seem to complain that they constantly need more information.

- The assumption that information from such formally constituted departments will be used ignores the dynamics of decision-making in organisations. Such departments are created on the assumption that managers will use the information from the beginning of any idea or project they may have. As will be demonstrated in chapter 2, decision-making in an organisation is highly influenced by internal social and political considerations and follows complex and convoluted processes of initiation, momentum-building and final acceptance. By the time the proposal reaches senior levels it has often already acquired too much momentum to be changed in any material way without there being serious consequences. When information is collected from such formally constituted information units it is often used to justify the decision which has already been made rather than contributing to the decision-making process.

  - Some units, particularly Strategic Business Units, are set up for the specific and exclusive use of senior managers and the Board. This is likely to create considerable friction among managers who do not have access to its work and yet who are responsible for doing a lot of the work which informs the Board; factors such as this are likely to ensure that the work of managers in this position is not informed by the work of such units, with the result that information provided by such a unit may cease to have any effect on decisions made throughout the rest of the organisation.

- Many units are set up without the commitment of most of the managers. They may pay lip-service to the setting up of such departments but still rely on their own sources of information about the environment. Indeed, a recent Reuters (1996) survey revealed that 44% of managers believed that the cost of collecting information exceeds its value to business.

- Managers often perceive people working in formally constituted information units as lacking in business understanding and/or experience and as such, managers are likely to regard the information provided by such departments as less important than information provided by a trusted peer or subordinate or boss. Indeed, Strategic Business Units, for instance, are often staffed by new MBAs on the fast track in the organisation and there may be some justification in the belief that their view of the business may be based on academic study rather than business experience.

- With few exceptions, the library is not well-regarded in organisations; only four out of 515 managers regard it as a useful source of information in a recent Reuters (1994) survey. One of the main reasons for this, according to McGee and Prusak (1992), may be that librarians often fail to take responsibility for the information which they provide and they often fail to interact with the decision-makers in the organisation. The information provided by members of a library is often delivered in a variety formats with little regard for its timeliness, accuracy or relevance; nor is its usefulness to the recipient likely to be considered, according to McGee and Prusak (1992). Such information is frequently context-free, with little if any attempt to add value to it by, for instance, by removing duplication, summarising the information or draw-ing charts and diagrams to make the information more accessible and comprehensible to the recipient. This failure to provide in-formation which is easy to assimilate and relevant to the manager's current tasks creates a negative image of librarians who are often perceived by managers as lacking intimate knowledge of business and as being more interested in the collection and storage of books and the maintenance of their stacks.

It is clear, therefore, that such units are frequently not successfully ad-dressing the problems of information provision in many organisations, but it is equally clear that managers require vast amounts of informa-tion to perform their tasks and achieve the aims of the business. In a recent Reuters survey (1996), for instance, 66% of managers in compa-nies of all sizes and within all departments claimed that they needed very high levels of information to perform effectively, 54% said they collected 'a great deal' of information to use in decision-making and 38% said they wasted substantial amounts of time trying to locate the information which they require.

Information systems

Much has been written about the problems which managers encounter in their use of information systems. To some extent the criticism cen-tres on the tendency of many organisations, until very recently, to regard the technology rather than the information as the primary issue of con-cern. This focus on the mediation of the information rather than the information itself resulted in two types of problems – those concern-ing the lack of provision of relevant information and those concerned with the technology.

Problems of information provision
- Usability of the information systems provided – many people complain that they receive too much data from information sys-tems and that the data which they receive is not in a usable form. They complain that the available reporting formats are not help-ful and that, at best, the reports which they receive are a compromise. According to McKinnon and Bruns (1992), most managers prefer to have facilities available to enable them to de-sign their own reports or at least have someone design them with their specific needs in mind. Similarly, as Mintzberg (1975) points out, formal information systems tend to aggregate data and, as a result, a lot of the available information is too general to be of much use. Designers of systems seem to believe that data must be aggregated in order not to swamp the manager with informa-tion but in doing so the data often ceases to be of use to the individual manager.
- Data integrity – Howard and Weinroth (1987) report that there is considerable disquiet about the integrity and reliability of data stored on some information systems which are often perceived as containing contradictory information. The enormous input

effort required to keep such systems up-to-date may cause or-ganisational problems and much of the data available in the systems is provided too late. This delay is caused by the neces-sity of inputting and aggregating the data and is often not required by managers. Important information which might trigger action by the practising manager, such as strike action by distributors or problems in a competing organisation, will take time to reach the system (if it ever does) and it is this kind of 'trigger' information which is vital to the successful functioning of the organisation.

Inevitably, the formal reporting structure in many organisations results in a considerable time-lag between the collection of the data and its appearance in a formal report on the manager's desk or on his screen. (Newer technologies such as groupware may alleviate some of these problems but for many organisations the lack of integrity of much of at least some of its data can create considerable problems.)

- Data collected – Crockett (1992) reports that managers often be-lieve that information systems are designed to collect that information which is easy to collect (for instance, quantitative data) while ignoring other potentially useful information because it is more difficult to collect. Crockett (1992) also reports that some managers believed that the data collected did not address the important issues of the business; rather, it was confined to the collection of what are often seen as surrogate measures of per-formance. Performance measures are obviously important but managers are also interested in qualitative information such as information about the organisation and group dynamics. Mintzberg (1975) agrees; he says that management information systems (MIS) produce valid information for unimportant and programmed (structured) problems and invalid information for important and non-programmed (unstructured) problems[1].

- Managers also believe that many information systems designers often fail to take account of the dynamic nature of the business. Howard and Weinroth (1987) report that managers believe that information systems are often built to serve the information needs of the organisation as defined at a specific point in time, but the business climate changes and when this happens the informa-tion which the organisation collects should also change. (Again, newer technologies which collect information as a by-product of production and other processes may alleviate this problem to some extent.)

Problems with the technology
- Compatibility of hardware – Users complain of problems of hard-ware incompatibility. It is often difficult to transfer data without hassle from one system to another. Similarly, there may be problems in transferring data designed for use in one system to another, thus data collected as part of the production processes may be awkward to transfer into office systems such as word processing and databases

applications. These problems may be alleviated to some extent when the organisation implements networked systems.

- Development of parallel systems – the perceived inadequacy of many centralised management information systems often results in the development of parallel systems. Managers who believe that their own needs are not being served by the organisation's central systems may design and build (or commission someone else to design and build) systems which reflect their own personal needs. Such action frequently results in a further deterioration of central systems since the need to support central systems is reduced and the submission of data to the centre will then carry a lower priority. Such dilution of the importance of the centralised system may become a vicious circle as others then develop their own parallel systems to counteract the increasing irrelevance of the central system. (Again, technologies such as groupware may alleviate this problem to some extent.)

- Lack of support from centre – many of the managers surveyed by Howard and Weinroth (1987) complained that they did not receive sufficient support. They complained that there were few training courses for users in how to deal with the data and there is little leadership provided to make people computer literate. Even when such problems are addressed, managers often believe that they receive little cooperation when they wish to make changes to the system and when changes are implemented managers complain that they take too long or are too late.

- Lack of access to external systems – users would like gateways to be provided to systems which offer external information.

- Problems of Executive Information Systems – even executive information systems (EIS) which are designed to address some of the problems of centralised management information systems are not ideal. Crockett (1992) suggests that the data they collect may help to diagnose problems within the organisation but this does not mean they can find solutions to the problems they identify. Managers often complain of the lack of linkages to other strategic functions which hamper the usefulness of such systems.

Technologies such as datawarehousing and groupware are making some managers more aware of the importance of information and how it can be manipulated and it seems probable that, in future, it will be the organisational requirement for information which will dictate the design of organisational information systems rather than the availability of technology. As managers become more informed about the opportunities and limitations of technology, and hence are in a better position to dictate the information architectures of their organisations, we can expect to see more organisations aligning information technology with their corporate strategy. If this happens, then the technology will become the enabler of many of the organisational processes, not merely an adjunct to its main functions as is currently the position in many organisations.

Communication barriers

Communication problems often hinder the flow of information within organisations. All organisations need to communicate and the formal channels of communication will often reflect organisational structure. There are three main types of communication in organisations, the use of one rather than another within the organisation will have a large influence on the flow of information within the organisation:

- One-way communication – often regarded as indicative of the traditional (old-fashioned) organisation, such one-way communication implies that information passes only from the management down to the workers. This style of communication has been vilified by some writers on management who suggest that it implies a dysfunctional organisation because no element of consultation or discussion is involved. To some extent this may be true, but such one-way communication may be entirely appropriate where issues such as health and safety rules are involved, for instance, where non-compliance might endanger the lives of the workers and result in prosecution for the organisation.

  In many organisations information is cascaded down through the hierarchies and within each hierarchy the manager advises the people for whom he/she is responsible and then those subordinates are expected to cascade the information to their subordinates. One-way communication may be in either written or verbal form; often initial oral communication is followed up by written material, frequently in the form of manuals, instructions, handbooks and newsletters.

- Two-way communication – this may take the form of communication from management and response by the workers or vice versa or may involve channels for new information to be communicated upwards. Again, information may be cascaded down but there will also be mechanisms for the upward communication of information; these may take the form of formal mechanisms such as consultative committees or less formal mechanisms such as chatting to the manager when he/she 'walks the job'. Two-way communication may be facilitated by the use of the so-called 'open-door' policy by the manager.

- Horizontal communication – in organisations with traditional functional boundaries some communication must be cross-functional and interdisciplinary. There will be much horizontal information processing in organisations which need to coordinate activities across functional boundaries in order to ensure that the organisation operates as a coordinated whole. The amount of information which is needed by each function will depend on the interdependence of the functions. In organisations where the traditional hierarchical structure has been replaced by one with flatter hierarchies which emphasise team-working, and where decisions are made at the point of need, communication of information will be largely horizontal.

In many organisations there are numerous facilities, such as notice boards and telephones, to aid the flow of information and many organisations make great use of meetings. In recent years new technologies such as email, groupware and videoconferencing have provided additional methods of communicating. The existence of communication facilities, however, does not guarantee that information will flow freely within the organisation. The culture and norms of the organisation may inhibit communication and such problems must be addressed if the free-flow of information is to be achieved.

While formal channels to facilitate the flow of information around the organisation may be in place, there are still likely to be barriers which prevent its free-flow. In organisations with a complex hierarchical structure where the flow of information is both up and down, no individual has all the necessary information with which to make a decision and this may result in a poor performance for the organisation as a whole.

There are also many interpersonal variables which may obstruct the free-flow of information around the organisation; some are caused by negligence, some by design, but many occur entirely by accident. A few examples are given below:

- Personal status – a person's status and title can act as a barrier to communication in the organisation. Junior staff may be reluctant to approach someone who seems to be very busy as they may believe that the person will not have time to see them, or may regard what they have to say as trivial. Personal demeanour may also create barriers to communication – some people give an impression of being unapproachable. Such a barrier may be created deliberately or by accident but the end-result is that crucial information may not be passed to people who need it and this may be detrimental to the organisation as a whole.

- Physical distance may also act as a barrier to communication – a person who works at some distance from head office may feel and act more autonomously and may be less likely to pass on information. Such a problem may be overcome to some extent by use of new technologies such as email, groupware and videoconferencing.

- Language barriers – many organisational divisions and hierarchies develop their own shorthand or jargon. Members of such divisions often lapse into this jargon when talking to those who have not been initiated and this will impede communication. They may believe they have communicated effectively but the receiver may have little understanding of what has been said and may feel inhibited or embarrassed to ask for an explanation, so the flow of information may be impeded.

- Perception barriers – different people in the organisation have differing perceptions of the organisation and its priorities. Managers often forget this and assume that everyone shares their viewpoint – this can cause considerable barriers to communication. For instance, management must have a holistic view of the organisation, whereas workers in an individual division see the organisation from a narrower departmental viewpoint. Indeed, organisations frequently encourage this narrower viewpoint by rewarding employees on the basis of their performance in their department rather than on the results of the organisation as a whole. Messages which assume a holistic viewpoint are thus likely to be ignored by individual workers as they are probably unable to understand their relevance.

- Sender's vantage point – it is quite common for communications in the organisation to be issued from the point of view of the sender rather than the receiver. Whenever a message is issued it must contain something to which the receiver can relate, otherwise the message may be misunderstood, not taken seriously, or even reinterpreted in the light of what the receiver expects to hear rather then what is actually said. For instance, a message advising the employees that their organisation is about to merge with another organisation might be perceived as excellent news for the organisation by the managers as it should bring more investment but without careful explanation such news might very easily be perceived by the workers as threatening job security.

- Non-verbal messages – the actions of an organisation may convey a much stronger message to its workers than what it says. Its actions may convey a message which can be used to reinforce a message or conversely detract from it. An organisation that professes that it welcomes suggestions from its employees but by its actions indicates that such suggestions are not valued will find that the well of new suggestions quickly dries up. Similarly, when an organisation says it welcomes risk-takers and then fires the person who takes a risk and fails, will soon find that risk-taking activity within the organisation declines to nothing.

- Hierarchies – the more hierarchies through which the message has to pass, the greater the chance that the message will be distorted in some way as it passes through the human filters. Organisations using the cascade method of communication may have particular problems. In principle, cascading information seems to be an efficient and personal way of disseminating information but there are several problems with this approach. Firstly, there is distortion and loss of quality of the message as each filter in the hierarchy reinterprets what has been said, secondly there is much wastage as everyone in the organisation gets a common message rather than a message that is geared to their needs and one to which they will find it easy to relate.

- Information technology – the very media used to disseminate the information may act as a barrier to communication. People need to be trained on how to make effective use of the technology; different media are appropriate for different types of communication and care must be taken that the correct system is used for each communication act.

- Presentation of the message – care must be taken to present information in as easily understandable a manner as possible. This may involve the sender in extra work but should ensure that the receiver comprehends the message. Managers must understand that few employees will take the time to read lengthy documents. It is preferable to provide a short summary of the contents which can be easily assimilated and understood but which refers them to the longer document for the details. Where possible, lists of figures should be avoided and instead facilities such as graphics, which are easier to assimilate, should be employed. Where a message is complicated it may be appropriate to deliver a verbal presentation outlining the facts and allowing questions. This may be followed up by a written document which gives more details.

- Timing – the timing of communications is very important. If a communication is not timely it may well be ignored as it does not seem to be relevant to the job in hand. Similarly, the contents of a message may be missed if it is received at the same time as another message the contents of which is perceived as more important. This latter point has not been lost on the political spin-doctors who often issue bad news at a time to coincide with other news which they know the media will perceive to be more important and of more interest to the public.

- Negativism and cynicism – the urgency and importance attached to messages will tend to be regarded with cynicism if many messages are sent out as urgent. 'Urgent' messages will also lose their effect when nothing happens as a result of their being sent. Thus, where people are asked for their opinion but it is not acted upon, they will be more reluctant to take the time to give their opinion in the future and may react with cynicism when asked to participate in other ways in the organisation. People are also likely to be wary of what they regard as the duplicitous nature of some messages – where information collected for one purpose is possibly going to be used against them.

Informal communication channels which bypass the formal channels are frequently a more efficient and effective method of information collection and processing. Informal methods of communication include conversations over lunch in the staff restaurant or staff common room; these may take the form of gossip, hearsay or speculation or represent a genuine exchange of facts. Other methods of informal communication may include post-it notes stuck on desks, email and, perhaps most important of all, the organisational grapevine. Many organisations realise that such exchange of information is very important and may place coffee machines at frequent intervals in the organisation, thus encouraging the exchange of information as people congregate to take refreshment. Open-plan offices may also encourage the exchange of information.

EFFECTS OF THE NEW TECHNOLOGIES ON ORGANISATIONS

The availability and flow of information within the organisation has been greatly facilitated by the introduction of new technology. Few organisations have come to terms with the enormous effects that the new information and communications technologies will have on their methods of production, information processing, and decision-making. It seems clear, however, that as Drucker (1988) indicates, within twenty years most organisations will be knowledge-based. This will have a profound effect not only on the way organisations operate but also on their structure. For instance, many organisations have used the new technologies to facilitate a switch from a functional to a process orientation. Traditional departmental boundaries have been broken down and a flatter organisational structure has developed together with a more team-based approach to work.

The new information and communication technologies are also having a huge impact on the collection of information, and the delivery of business intelligence and, as a result, the quality and speed of decision-making should improve. Many managers are familiar with email, image transmission and videoconferencing, but to these can now be added much more sophisticated tools such as expert systems, document management systems, datawarehousing, groupware and intranets. Such devices will enable the manager to store, organise, retrieve, manipulate and disseminate information much more efficiently, quickly and effectively. For instance, large numbers of people dispersed across the globe can be sent the same information simultaneously, and the information can be discussed using videoconferencing and manipulated and stored. New technologies enable the organisation to record all communication events (telephone calls, meetings etc.) without the distortion of written minutes which should facilitate the rapid, accurate identification of problems and opportunities so that further data acquisition can be more focused.

The use of these new tools is changing the organisations themselves and the tasks in which they engage. Indeed, in some industries the new technology has completely changed the way the business itself is done. For instance, trading on the London Stock Exchange is now carried out electronically. In some industries the new technologies have created new methods with which to compete – many retail stores now offer a loyalty card which enables them to capture data about their customers' spending habits as well as providing incentives directly to the customers to remain loyal. In other industries, as Porter and Miller (1985) point out, the technology has created new types of business as a direct spin-off of the collection of information.

The new technologies have also enabled managers to make better use of the data which already exists in the organisation. It is now possible to integrate previously discrete techniques and information isolated on decentralised systems into one corporate information system. This makes possible new ways of using the data, diagnosing problems, seeking out opportunities and making decisions. Thus, information can be used in a radically new way – it can be used as a measurement on which to base future action rather than as a post mortem and a record of what has already happened. Technologies such as datawarehousing, for instance, enable the managers to mine deep into data from many different sources and manipulate it to identify trends and correlations which were not previously apparent, or to see the business in different ways, or to identify business opportunities which were not previously obvious. Technology has also had a large impact on the more traditional functions such as finance; for instance, the new tools have enabled a shift from traditional cost accounting to activity based costing. Manufacturing has also been affected, the new technologies permit the measuring and collecting of information about every detail of the process and its raw materials. Such information provides the basis for more efficient and effective resource allocation, thus cutting costs and improving the organisation's competitive position.

In some organisations the new technologies have been used as the basis on which to re-engineer the business. The result of this has often been a huge improvement in profitability as well as a large improvement in the efficiency and effectiveness of organisational information processing.

BUSINESS PROCESS RE-ENGINEERING AND THE FLOW OF INFORMATION

Developed by Hammer and Champy and reported in 1993, business process re-engineering (BPR) reorganises the corporation around customers and reduces functional specialisation and activities which add little or no value to the customer. The technique realigns the organisation around a number of business processes – a process is a set of activities that taken together produce a result of value to the customer. Re-engineering usually results in a radical change in the shape and character of the organisation and it is usually technology that enables this re-engineering. The results of re-engineering are often dramatic improvements in performance measures such as cost, service, quality and speed. Re-engineering usually breaks down the barriers between functional fiefdoms; indeed, it usually does away with fiefdoms altogether by combining what previously had been several jobs into one. Consequently, it usually has a considerable impact on the flow of information within the organisation. The lack of barriers means that information flows more easily both vertically and horizontally. After a re-engineering exercise, workers are usually given more responsibility to ensure that customers needs are met, and they are usually given more authority to make decisions, so there is less need to report upwards. Similarly, there is little or no need to have meetings with other departments to solve problems because after BPR there are fewer functional divisions and problems are often solved as part of the normal business process. So, the flatter hierarchy which is produced as a result of the re-engineering process means that there are fewer levels through which information needs to flow, and the change in the way work is performed results in less need for information to flow since decisions are made at a lower level. As a result of BPR, therefore, there are usually fewer barriers to the communication of information but also less information that needs to flow.

INTELLECTUAL CAPITAL AND THE RISE OF THE LEARNING ORGANISATION

At the same time as the problems of information and its management have gained centre-stage in many organisations, there has also been a recognition of the importance of knowledge. As we have seen, Drucker (1988) has commented on the pre-eminence of knowledge-based organisations in the next century and interest is now beginning to focus on the concept of fostering knowledge creation and development by building a learning organisation and by cultivating the learning organisation's most important asset – intellectual capital.

As more people in an organisation spend their time handling ideas and information, methods must be devised to deal with the knowledge created and the problems highlighted by this new asset: intellectual capital. Intellectual capital is difficult to define but may be regarded as the wisdom and knowledge within the organisation which can be harnessed to improve the competitive position of the company. 'Intellectual capital,' to quote Stewart (1997) 'is packaged useful knowledge'. Each worker who handles ideas and information contributes to the total of the intellectual capital within the organisation. In many organisations, most of the workers are engaged in information handling – even those jobs which might previously have been regarded as manual often involve information handling. This is most evident where production processes have been automated and the erstwhile shop-floor workers spend their time monitoring the process in which relevant data is collected automatically as a by-product of the production process.

Problems created by intellectual capital

Knowledgeable workers are in demand and are highly mobile and, as the knowledge they possess is such an important asset in the organisation, the loss of one such worker may reflect adversely on the company in the same way as the loss of any other asset. Few organisations are comfortable knowing that they must rely for their success on something over which they have so little control as their staff. It is therefore understandable that there should be so much interest in the creation and development of a learning organisation, where individual information and knowledge are shared across the organisation and where loyalty is fostered by a shared vision of the successful organisation, in which everyone has a role to play and all can share in its success.

Fostering the development of intellectual capital

A learning organisation is one which recognises the importance of its intellectual capital and ensures that it is constantly renewed by providing opportunities for individual learning. A learning organisation creates systems and relationships to ensure that individual learning is leveraged to the whole organisation to meet its goals and objectives. The managers of a learning organisation try to ensure that all opportunities for learning are used and such learning is leveraged throughout the organisation; for instance, details of an improved method of doing something or new solutions to problems will be widely disseminated, and a customer complaint received in one section of the organisation may be used to stimulate discussion on how to improve service throughout the whole organisation. Individual expertise may also be made widely available to the organisation in the form of expert systems or online databases – Microsoft Inc. has encapsulated the knowledge of its best engineers in a database and made this available to workers on its helpdesk so they are better able to help customers.

The managers of a learning organisation recognise that they must harness the abilities and the commitment of all their workers if they are to succeed and so they encourage their workforce to read widely. Some of the learning material which they make available to their employees may seem to have little bearing on the mainstream business of the organisation but the management believes that exposure to non-standard material may help the individual to see the environment from a different perspective and hence enable the him/her to provide more creative solutions to the problems of the organisation. More importantly, however, the learning organisation recognises that reading alone is not sufficient; it is discussion with others which facilitates learning and knowledge and so the management may equip staff rooms and conference rooms with white boards and other facilities to encourage the creation and sharing of knowledge and the free-flow of information. To improve its stock of intellectual capital, the learning organisation usually fosters teamwork and creates communities of practice in which constant improvement and learning take place and it may encourage many other forms of formal and informal learning and discussion.

Problems of managing intellectual capital

The rise of the knowledge worker often causes problems for the organisation, however. The productivity of such a person is difficult to measure – the value of a good idea to the organisation is probably incalculable – one bright idea might transform the company's ability to compete and add millions to its share value yet might be the product of only one morning's work. The rise of the knowledge worker also makes the valuation of the company more difficult – you cannot value the abilities of the workforce. In Microsoft Inc., for example, the value of the company is not in the number of factories but in the skills and abilities of the workers – the physical capital is not worth nearly as much as these. Some intellectual assets, such as patents and copyrights, can be measured but the vast majority cannot. Handy (1989) estimates that the intellectual assets of a company are usually worth three to four times the tangible book value.

Further problems are created because the organisation needs knowledge workers but they are in high demand and may only stay loyal to the organisation while it provides them with ample resources and interesting projects on which to work. This may be difficult to achieve in adverse economic circumstances but failure to do so may result in an exodus of valuable workers leaving the company in an even worse competitive position.

Making the transition to a learning organisation

The managers of a learning organisation recognise that in a dynamic business only organisations which can adapt quickly will survive, and they believe that learning acts as both a catalyst for change and also a means by which such change can be driven within the organisation.

Clearly, the creation of an environment in which information and knowledge is leveraged is likely to be advantageous to the business but other factors are also driving organisations towards their re-birth as learning organisations. The transition from a traditional organisation to a learning organisation is a difficult one to make, however. The requirement that information and learning must be shared virtually dictates a flat organisational structure, systems thinking, team-working and a culture of cooperation rather than competition among its members. Such a culture which encourages the creation and sharing of information may be alien to those who have always believed that 'knowledge is power' and that to share it is to dilute one's power – this may cause problems in the initial stages. There are also other equally fundamental problems: knowledge is often ephemeral, it is frequently situational or personal and certainly intangible and invisible; how can one create an organisation which has at its core something which is so difficult to define and indeed quantify? The transition to a learning organisation cannot be made by simply training individuals since training by its very nature tends to formalise organisational procedures and rules, thus stultifying the very creativity which the organisation is seeking to encourage.

For some organisations it is the information and communication technologies which have provided the impetus for their transition to a learning organisation. As was indicated above, the new technologies enable the organisation to capture and disseminate information in a wide variety of ways, including video, multimedia, groupware, intranets and email. Information collected may be about production processes, competitor intelligence, customers, suppliers, standards and news. As a result the organisation is able to create in-house yellow pages of corporate expertise, directories of relevant information and vast databases of industry and organisationally specific information linked together with copious cross-referencing. Even information contained in phone calls and emails can be routinely captured, stored and made available for use when required. However, it is not the information and communication technologies, nor even, ultimately, the information captured which are important, rather it is the use which the organisation makes of this and other material which will determine whether the organisation may be regarded as a learning organisation. Data and information by themselves do not create knowledge, knowledge comes when the individual sees the relationships and the contexts for that information and can create new patterns of thinking.

To facilitate knowledge creation and learning processes many organisations now use their own information to provide simulations of their business to help managers develop insights and skills, and to provide them with the opportunity to see the business from the perspective of another specialism. Such simulations also enable managers to try out different scenarios, make mistakes and see the consequences of their actions without having to incur those consequences, all within the context of their own organisation.

An organisation which aspires to become a leaning organisation will ultimately create and disseminate information and knowledge as natural by-product of working and will provide opportunities for all workers to contribute to the organisational store of knowledge.

CONCLUSION

The success or otherwise of the organisation depends on the efficient and effective use of the resources at its disposal, and this cannot be achieved without the processing of appropriate information and its flow to appropriate individuals and functions.

Some organisations have dealt with what they perceive as a problem of information flow among individual departments and functions by re-engineering their business to a more process- rather then function-based organisation, thus enhancing the information flows. Others have fostered the creation of an 'information' culture within the organisation in which the importance of information and its successful processing is recognised as essential to the successful functioning of the organisation. Such a culture should enhance the flow of information around the organisation and foster a recognition among individual members of the organisation that quality of information is more important than its quantity. The development of such a culture should ensure that it will be the nature of the information processing rather than the requirements of the technology which will determine the organisation's information architecture.

It is clear, however, that many organisations now recognise the pivotal role which information and its processing plays in their organisation. Many such organisations are already knowledge-based and recognise the value of their intellectual capital, and it is likely that many others will make the transition to fully-fledged learning organisations very soon. To fail to do so might severely jeopardise their competitive position with serious consequences for both the organisation and its workers.

BIBLIOGRAPHY

Abell, Angela. 'Information Use and Business Success: a review of recent research of effective information delivery,' in *The Value and Impact of Information*, edited by Mary Feeney and Maureen Grieves (East Grinstead: Bowker-Saur, 1994).

Aguilar, Francis Joseph. *Scanning the Business Environment* (New York: Macmillan, 1967).

Clippinger, John H. 'Visualisation of Knowledge: building and using intangible assets digitally.' *Planning Review*, November/December 1995, pp. 28-31, 46.

Corzine, R. 'Business and the Environment: Shell and that sinking feeling.' *Financial Times*, 5 July 1995, p. 14.

Crockett, Fess. 'Revitalizing Executive Information Systems.' *Sloan Management Review*, Summer 1992, pp. 39-47.

Daft, Richard L. and Lengel, Robert H. 'Information Richness: a new approach to managerial behaviour and organisational design.' *Research in Organisational Behaviour* 6, 1984, pp. 191-233.

Drucker, Peter. 'The Coming of the New Organisation.' *Harvard Business Review* 1, 1988, pp. 45-53.

Drucker, Peter. 'The Information Executives Truly Need.' *Harvard Business Review*, January/February 1995, pp. 54-62.

Feldman, Martha S. and March, James G. 'Information in Organisations as Signal and Symbol.' *Administrative Science Quarterly* 26, 1981, pp. 171-186.

Ghoshal, Sumantra and Kim, Seok Ki. 'Building Effective Intelligence Systems for Competitive Advantage.' *Sloan Management Review*, Fall 1986, pp. 49-58.

Hammer, Michael and Champy, James. *Re-engineering the Corporation: a manifesto for business revolution* (London: Nicholas Brealey, 1993).

Handy, C. *The Age of Unreason* (London: Business Books, 1989).

Howard, Geoffrey S. and Weinroth, G. Jay. 'Users' Complaints: information system problems from the users' perspective.' *Journal of Systems Management*, May 1987, pp. 30-34.

Huber, George P. 'A Theory of the Effects of Advanced Information Technologies on Organisational Design, Intelligence and Decision making.' *Academy of Management Review* 15, 1990, pp. 47-71.

Larson, Erik W. and King, Jonathan B. 'The Systematic Distortion of Information: an ongoing challenge to management.' *Organisational Dynamics*, 1992, pp. 49-61.

McGee, James V. and Prusak, Laurence. *Managing Information Strategically* (New York: John Wiley & Sons, 1992).

McKinnon, Sharon M. and Bruns, William J. *The Information Mosaic* (Boston: Harvard Business School Press, 1992).

Mintzberg, Henry. *Impediments to Use of Management Information* (New York and Hamilton, Ontario: National Association of Accountants and The Society of Industrial Accountants of Canada, 1975).

Pettinger, Richard. *Introduction to Organisational Behaviour* (Basingstoke: Macmillan, 1996).

Porter M. and Miller, V. 'How Information Gives You a Competitive Advantage.' *Harvard Business Review,* July/August 1985, pp. 149-160.

Reuters Business Research. *To Know or Not to Know: the politics of information* (London: Reuters, 1994).

Reuters Business Research. *Dying for Information* (London: Reuters, 1996).

Schneider, Susan C. 'Information Overload: causes and consequences.' *Human Systems Management 7,* 1987, pp. 143-153.

Senge, Peter. *The Fifth Discipline* (London: Century Business, 1990).

Stewart, Thomas A. *Intellectual Capital: the new wealth of nations* (London: Nicholas Brealey, 1997).

Taylor, Robert S. *Value-added Processes in Information Systems* (Norwood: Ablex Publishing, 1986).

Tushman, Michael L. and Nadler, David A. 'Information Processing as an Integrating Concept in Organisational Design.' *Academy of Management Review,* 1978, pp. 613-624.

Notes

1   For further discussion of programmed and non-programmed problems see chapter 3.

Chapter 2

What do managers do?

INTRODUCTION

The successful provision of information to managers to enable them to perform their tasks requires an understanding of the tasks which managers perform in the organisation and the nature of their role in the environment external to that organisation, because it is these factors which will determine their need (or otherwise) for information.

Much has been written on the nature of the management role and the tasks which the manager performs. However, a precise definition of management has proved to be illusory. Henry Fayol, in the early years of the century, defined the management process as 'forecasting, planning, organising, commanding, coordinating and controlling', whilst Luther Gulick used the acronym PODSCORB (planning, organising, directing, staffing, coordinating, reporting and budgeting) to describe the managerial tasks. Later writers such as Mintzberg (1973, 1975) were to demonstrate that while such tasks might be deemed to be the rightful tasks of managers, few managers actually conformed to type – the difference between what managers were supposed to do and what they actually did was shown to be considerable and resulted in a rethink of the nature of managerial roles and tasks. Consequently later writers have taken a more general approach: Tom Peters (1992) defined management as 'organisational direction based on sound common sense, pride in the organisation and enthusiasm for its works'.

For many people, however, the phrase 'getting things done through other people' provides a useful guide to what management is about. This phrase is not, however, sufficiently explicit to provide a useful foundation on which to base decisions about the provision of appropriate information to managers. What is clear, however, is that few people still regard management as *merely* common sense; the idea that managers are born and cannot be made seems largely to have disappeared and the popularity of management and business courses at both undergraduate and postgraduate level bears testimony to a general recognition that management is a body of knowledge, aptitudes and skills which can be learnt and which must be regarded as a prerequisite for managers of organisations which wish to survive and prosper in the next century. What is equally clear is that it is the manner in which managers combine their knowledge, personal characteristics, skills and experience which will determine the success or otherwise of the organisation. It is appropriate, therefore, to look in greater detail at these factors and to identify, where possible, any common attributes that good managers possess and then to look at any propositions which can be made about the nature of the managerial tasks and the way in which the manager performs them before discussing their information needs.

THE PERCEIVED REQUIREMENTS FOR SUCCESSFUL MANAGEMENT

Management skills

If a manager is to be able to accomplish tasks through other people, it is imperative that those performing in a management role should be good communicators in both written and verbal forms with people inside their own organisation such as subordinates, peers and superiors as well as stakeholders external to the organisation, such as clients, customers, peers and suppliers. The ability to build teams and to motivate people must be regarded as important management skills together with a keen understanding of human motivators and human behaviour.

Managerial personality

To perform successfully in the managerial role and carry out the related tasks, the manager needs a variety of personal qualities; these include ambition, energy, great commitment, self-motivation, job, product and service knowledge, drive, enthusiasm and creativity and imagination. The dynamic nature of the business environment requires that the manager must be able to adapt to change and be alert to changes in the business environment, so a thirst for knowledge and a commitment to continuing personal and professional development, coupled with considerable self-discipline, are essential.

Decision-making is one of the most important aspects of management and so managers must be able to make unpalatable decisions with limited information. A manager must also be able to lead other people; he/she must be able to enthuse others and galvanise them into action to ensure that progress is made towards the achievement of the aims and objectives of the organisation – getting results through other people.

Management knowledge and education

There is no recognised legal requirement for managers to be formally educated in management, though many managers follow courses leading to the award of a formal qualification such as an MBA. Nor, indeed, is there a recognised body of knowledge that is recognised as exclusively 'management'; however, there is a vague consensus among many managers and those responsible for their education concerning which areas of knowledge should constitute the management curriculum:

- Organisations – managers need to have some understanding about the factors governing the structure and functioning of organisations and their relationships with the external environment.

- Finance and budgeting – financial resources are in short supply and need to be accounted for. The manager must be aware of the financial techniques which will ensure that the limited resources available are used in the best way. This includes not only careful budgeting but also techniques such as evaluating capital investments, cash flow management and debt management.

- Information – managers must be able to collect, store, organise, manipulate and disseminate information effectively and they must understand the importance of information to their organisation and ensure that information flows effectively around the organisation. The effective management of information is likely to be a major determinant of organisational success in the future.

- Information Technology (IT) – an appropriate information architecture is vital to the continued survival and prosperity of the organisation. The manager must understand how IT can be harnessed to fulfil the aims and objectives of the organisation and the importance of aligning IT to corporate strategy. Managers must be familiar with both the information systems and the organisation's requirements for information and they must be able to use the information effectively. They must be able to ask for appropriate information and present it in ways the members of the organisation can use.

- Economics and current affairs – managers must possess a knowledge of the financial and trading climate as it affects the business.

- Law and the regulatory framework – this will include details of the law governing trade and the manufacture and sale of goods, health and safety and employment legislation, together with an understanding of the law as it affects trade.

- Planning – all managers need an understanding of the techniques of strategy formulation and policy making.

- Performance measurement – managers must be able to work to deadlines and within resource constraints. They must set standards of performance for themselves and their peers, their subordinates and the organisation as a whole and take steps to remedy that performance when it falls below the standards set.

- Human resource management – a knowledge of what motivates people and how they should be rewarded, coupled with a knowledge of industrial relations and salary policies.

- Operations management – for many managers an understanding of the principles and practices underlying operation and production management is vital.

- Facilities management – the correct management of facilities such as buildings, reprographics and warehousing may not be exciting but the facilities form part of the infrastructure of the organisation and may cause considerable problems if left untended and unmanaged.

- Marketing and sales – an in-depth knowledge of the principles and practices governing the sale and marketing of products is essential for successful management.

- Quantitative and analytical methods – managers require knowledge of analytical and quantitative methods to enable them to recognise those activities which are likely to be profitable, and to determine the most effective and efficient methods of doing business.

- Project management – projects form an important part of the activity of most organisations – they may take the form of research and development projects, projects to launch a new product, to enter a new market or build and equip a new factory. Whatever the type of project it will need to be managed to ensure that the resources are used effectively and efficiently and can be accounted for. Project management knowledge is required to ensure that the project is completed on time and that systems are in place to monitor its success.

Others areas now appearing in the management curriculum include the management of innovation, knowledge management and entrepreneurship.

Management tasks and activities

There is considerable discussion of the activities which constitute management. Indeed, anything which impinges on the interests of the organisation might be said to be of concern to management and hence a possible candidate for inclusion in a list of such activities. However, a few general statements can be made about such tasks and activities:

- The organisation of staff into productive teams and departments – it is the job of a manager to create teams to progress the organisation as a whole to the successful completion of its aims and objectives. This requires that the manager engenders feelings of esprit de corps and common purpose.

- Developing people – the dynamic nature of business means that a successful company must constantly innovate and change and this implies that managers must ensure that employees are not only trained to cope with the changes but are encouraged to develop as individuals and team members. Developing people means that they should be equipped to make original contributions to the organisation in excess of what might be expected from traditional training.

- Create and maintain standards – the manager will set the standards in many areas of the organisation. His/her personal qualities will determine ethical standards for such things as honesty and integrity within the organisation. Managers bring their own attitudes and values to the job and these will set the tone for subordinates. Providing and nurturing the correct attitudes is an essential part of the managerial tasks. The manager must provide a clear lead about maintaining standards.

- Determining and monitoring performance levels – the manager must set out clearly what is regarded as acceptable behaviour and he/she must demonstrate that deviation from such standards must not only be stopped but must be seen to be stopped. Managers must set out precisely what the aims and objectives of the organisation are and he/she should ensure that there is a control mechanism in place to ensure that those standards are met. Accountability must be clearly delineated and systems set in place to ensure that feedback on performance is easily available. The aims and objectives set should be challenging but attainable and should act as a motivator to all concerned. The objectives should be measurable and understood by all staff and the manager should ensure that everyone is committed to them.

- Provide vision – there should be a vision of the organisation's future direction and the path required to ensure that the organisation achieves that vision. It is a vision with which the manager can motivate more junior members of staff.

- Preventing and stopping conflict – conflict arises in most organisations; it might be a simple clash of personalities or a disagreement about working practices which sets managers against those who work operationally. A manager must be able to anticipate such conflict and should be equipped with sufficient negotiating skills to be able to defuse the situation and find a solution.

- Leading the people involved in the organisation – managers are required to provide leadership.

- Motivating people – managers are required to motivate employees.

- Coping with and managing change – most organisations are in state of constant change and many people find coping with change very difficult. The manager must be able to manage the change in such a way that people understand why such change is necessary, how it will affect them and what the organisation will do to help them cope with the change. Failure to manage change can cause considerable problems in the organisation.

- Crisis management – managers must be able to handle crises in such a way that stakeholder confidence is maintained in the organisation. He/she must be able to resolve dilemmas and conflicts relating to the organisational, departmental and individual aims and objectives, technology, production, marketing, economic, social, political and ethical factors and the wider relationship between the organisation and the external environment which will include customers and suppliers. The manager must seek to identify, address and resolve problems and conflict within the organisation.

- Negotiation – managers are required to engage in negotiations with those internal to the organisation and also with suppliers, customers and others.

- Decision making – much management activity involves decision-making.

- Planning – a manager must initiate and develop policy and strategy.

- Discipline and grievance – managers must have policies to deal with disciplinary and grievance issues and be able to handle such problems in a manner which is fair and is perceived to be fair.

- Resource allocation and budgeting – resources are in short supply and the manager must ensure that all resources are allocated in the most effective and efficient manner and that systems are in place to ensure that such resources can be accounted for. Budgets must be set for all areas, such as staff, production, outputs, operational costs, administrative expenditure and other facilities.

MINTZBERG'S PROPOSITIONS ABOUT MANAGERIAL WORK

In 1973 Mintzberg published a book which contained what he referred to as propositions about the nature of managerial work. After extensive investigations into what managers actually do, as opposed to what management writers believed that they should do, Mintzberg reported that little had changed about managerial work in 100 years. He also noted that the ways in which managers work are similar across industrial sectors and across all levels of the organisation. He made the following propositions about the nature of managerial work:

- The managerial job is open-ended; there are lots of tasks which need to be performed, so managers tend to perform a great deal of work at an unrelenting pace. Time is in such short supply that work occupies most of their time, they have little free time and usually take work home.

- Contrary to the popular conception of managerial work, it is characterised by brevity, variety, fragmentation and interruption. The vast majority of activities which the manager performs are of brief duration – often only a few seconds or minutes. There is great variety and little pattern to what the manager does and the trivial tasks are interspersed with the more important tasks, so the manager needs to be able to re-orient him/herself quickly and frequently. Superficiality is an occupational hazard of the manager's job.

- It may seem strange to many people, but the manager seems to prefer brevity and interruptions in his/her work. He/she is conditioned to the workload and lives continuously with an awareness of those other tasks which might or must be achieved at any one time.

- The manager seems to prefer the more active elements of the work – the current, the specific, the well-defined, the non-routine. Routine events such as processing the mail are disliked and viewed as a burden.

- Managers show a distinct preference for verbal rather than written information. There is a strong preference for very current information such as gossip and hearsay while long reports and formal communications frequently go unheeded.

- The pressure of work, the number of specific issues and the complexity of managerial work result in less time for planning than traditional management writers have suggested. Indeed, the pressure and complexity of their work encourages the development of the manager whom Mintzberg (1973) describes as a person who is an '... adaptive information manipulator who works in a stimulus response environment and who favours live action.'

- Many managers also spend some time touring the organisation to directly observe its activities informally.

- Managers spend a lot of time in meetings; external contacts consume about a third of contact time and a great variety of people such as clients, suppliers, associates, peers and others are involved. Such contacts form a network which the manager uses to provide information. Subordinates consume about a third to one half of the manager's contact time; such meetings are used most frequently for the purposes of making requests or sending or receiving information and making strategy. The manager interacts freely with a variety of subordinates often bypassing formal channels of communication. Only about 10% of a manager's time is spent with his superiors.

MINTZBERG'S PROPOSITIONS ABOUT THE MANAGERIAL ROLE

Mintzberg (1973) suggests that managerial roles may be grouped into three categories – those concerned primarily with interpersonal relationships, those concerned with information processing and those that involve the making of significant decisions – and that these categories may be further divided into 10 observable roles:

- Managerial roles involving interpersonal relationships:
  - figurehead – the manager must carry out a variety of legal, inspirational and ceremonial duties;
  - liaison – in liaison with others the manager builds up a substantial network of contacts and information is traded for mutual benefit;
  - leader – in this role the manager defines the work environment of subordinates, motivates them, trains them and ensures that their abilities are harnessed to achieve the aims and objectives of the organisation. This role pervades almost all management activity.

- Managerial roles involving information processing – Mintzberg suggests that the manager is the 'nerve centre' of the organisation's information. He has unique access to subordinates who supply information as well as having access to the vast network of external contacts as a result of the liaison role. Such contacts are themselves nerve centres in their own organisations. As a consequence, the manager develops a powerful database of external and internal information. These information processing roles include:

- monitor – as a monitor, the manager receives information on a wide variety of topics: internal operations, external events, trends, markets, competitors, ideas and opportunities. Such information may be specifically sought or may arrive unsolicited. The information is used to detect changes, identify problems and opportunities, to build up a general understanding of the business environment, and to inform decision-making and planning.

- disseminator – as a disseminator the manager sends external information into the organisation and internal information from one subordinate to another. This information may be factual or evaluative in nature.

- spokesperson – as spokesperson the manager transmits information about the organisation to external groups. The manager may operate in a public relations capacity; he may also lobby for the interests of the organisation. In this role the manager also acts as an expert in the field in which the organisation operates.

- Managerial roles involving decision-making – this involves many of the activities of the organisation including strategy determination. The roles include:

  - entrepreneur – in this capacity the manager searches for opportunities and problems, and designs and implements change. Most managers supervise several such projects at any one time.

  - disturbance handler – in a dynamic environment conflicts and disturbances are inevitable; the manager assumes the role of trouble-shooter on such occasions.

  - resource allocator – the manager decides what needs to be done and when and who will perform each task. This is achieved by retaining control over resource allocation and authorising all significant decisions. By this means the manager is able to integrate all significant decisions.

  - negotiator – in the role of negotiator the manager takes charge when the organisation must engage in important negotiation activity with other organisations. He participates as figurehead, as spokesman and as a resource allocator.

This division of roles is useful for analytical purposes but in reality it is very difficult to provide such a clear delineation. The manager may be performing several different roles at any one time, for instance, when he/she is both giving and receiving information in a meeting. However, while Mintzberg (1973) pointed out that all managers perform all these tasks, there are some variations in the amount and extent to which each of these tasks form part of their duties.

MINTZBERG'S PROPOSITIONS ABOUT VARIATIONS IN THE NATURE OF MANAGERIAL WORK

Mintzberg (1973) reports that he closely observed and questioned managers from all levels of a wide variety of organisations and his research indicated that all managers, from the chief executive to the most junior manager and across all organisations in all sectors, including both private and public, perform similar tasks. He went on to point out, however, that the precise proportion in which these tasks occupy the individual manager will depend on such factors as:

- environmental variables – the nature of the organisation and the situation in which the organisation finds itself at a particular time, together with the industrial sector in which the organisation is situated;
- job variables – the level of the manager in the organisation and the function for which he/she is responsible;
- the individual manager's personality and style;
- situational variables – such as the problems and events which are currently of paramount importance. For example, periods of threat require the manager to spend a great proportion of his/her time in the disturbance handler role, which is then followed by the replenishment of contacts and resources.

Mintzberg referred to these factors as contingent variables. He pointed out that his research demonstrated that the level of the job and the function supervised appear to account for more of the variation in managers' work than any other variables. The more dynamic the environment in which the manager works (this will include factors such as competition, rate of change, growth, and pressure to produce) the more time he/she will spend in information communication, and the more varied and fragmented will be his/her work and the greater his/her orientation to live action and to verbal media.

He further reported that managers at the top of organisations in the public sector spend more time in formal activity such as scheduled meetings and more time meeting directors and outside groups than do managers of private organisations. Top managers of service organisations spend more time in the liaison role than do those of product organisations.

Managers of small firms spend more time in the roles of specialist and substitute operator, whereas the larger the organisation the more time the top manager spends in formal communications (memos, scheduled meetings) and the less brief and fragmented his/her activities. A top manager of a large organisation will have a greater range of external contacts and a more developed formal communications network but there will be less involvement with internal operations and less time spent in substituting for subordinates.

The higher the level of the manager in the hierarchy the more unstructured, unspecialised and long-range will be the job, and the more intertwined, extended and complicated will be the issues with which he/she is required to deal. The lower the level, the more informal the job and the less time spent in the figurehead role. At the lower levels in organisations, many managers report that their main task is to ensure a steady workflow, so they spend more time than those at the top of the organisation in the roles of disturbance handler and negotiator. The lower the level, the more pronounced the characteristics of brevity and fragmentation and the greater the focus on the current and on specific issues.

CATEGORIES OF MANAGEMENT ACTIVITY

While Mintzberg's work concerning the nature of management (1973) has been much quoted, he does not report in much detail how this impacts on the manager's need for information. For such an explanation it is helpful to look to Anthony's work published in 1965 and to which Mintzberg (and several other writers) also refer. Anthony (1965) suggests that managerial activity can very basically be divided into three categories:

• operational control activity;

• activity associated with managerial and tactical control;

• strategic activity.

For each these categories of activity the manager acts as a monitor – he/she receives information which is used to detect changes, identify problems, detect trends and develop a better understanding of the organisation and its environment, but as Gorry and Scott Morton (1971) explain, each type of managerial activity requires a different type of information which comes from differing sources and which is used a different way. In a book which considers the information requirements of managers, therefore, it is important to be clear about the differing types of managerial task since this has such bearing on the type of information which the manager will require.

Operational control activity

Operational activity is activity which is usually associated with production, facilities, purchasing, sales or logistics. Operational activity is well-defined and narrow in scope and tends to be largely physical; as a result the processes can often be directly observed. For instance, operational activity in production may be the manufacture of a particular part for a machine. The management of such activity, which is often referred to as operational control activity, is largely concerned with tasks rather than with people; Anthony (1965) defined such operational control activity as 'the process of assuring that specific tasks are carried out effectively and efficiently'.

Little or no judgement is required to be exercised by managers responsible for the control of operational activity since the tasks and goals of the operational function and the resources required to perform such activity have been delineated by those responsible for the management control activity. The focus is on the execution of the task. To manage operational control activities, information is required about the extent to which tasks and goals have been achieved and resources used effectively and efficiently. Consequently, the operational process is monitored regularly and the information is collected at very frequent intervals – sometimes hourly, certainly daily. Such information is vital for the successful control of the operational processes and is obtained almost entirely from internal sources.

Managerial and tactical control

Management control activity differs from operational control activity because, unlike the latter, it is concerned largely with getting things done through people. Anthony (1965) suggests that managerial control is 'the process by which managers assure that resources are obtained and used effectively and efficiently in the accomplishment of the organisation's objectives'.

As Anthony (1965) points out, management control can only take place within the context of objectives and policies which have been arrived at during the strategic planning process and when clear criteria have been set out by which the effectiveness and efficiency of the objectives have been set. The purpose of management control activity is to ensure efficient and effective performance of tasks. Information for management control is largely obtained from internal sources such as from summarised reports of the results of operational processes but some external information may be used.

Strategic activity

Anthony's final type of management activity is strategic activity. He defines such activity as 'the process of deciding on the objectives of the organisation, on changes in these objectives, on the resources used to attain these objectives and on the policies that are to govern the acquisition, use and disposition of these resources'.

Strategic activity involves an attempt to predict the future business environment and the organisation's place in it. Such activity involves the solution of problems which are complex and non-routine (unlike other business activity, much of which is routine). It requires managers to think is creative ways and thus, by its very nature, it is very difficult to appraise the success or otherwise of the strategic planning process other than with the benefit of hindsight – for instance, by considering the success or otherwise of the organisation itself. Unlike other management activities, strategic planning requires much information which is generated from sources largely external to the organisation since what is required is information concerning activities which are largely external to the organisation. Such information gathering about the external environment is referred to as environmental scanning and it is not always easy to gather such information.

These three categories of activity will form the framework within which managerial information requirements will be discussed in later chapters.

MANAGERIAL TASKS AND ROLES IN THE ORGANISATION OF THE 21ST CENTURY

Change characterises the external business environment of most organisations and the manager is responsible for ensuring that the organisation is able to adapt to these changes. Similarly, technology is changing the internal business environment; it is enabling the organisation to cut costs and improve productivity often by automating previously labour intensive jobs. It seems likely, therefore, that the nature of the manager's job must also change. Koch and Godden (1996) argue that new technologies coupled with a much more customer-focused approach to the market might enable some organisations to radically reduce the number of managers in the organisation. In a book uncompromisingly entitled *Managing Without Management*, Koch and Godden (1996) argue that most of the time managers pursue activities that have very little value to customers and therefore very little value to investors or any other non-management constituency. They explain that managers race around reacting to crises, finding out what has gone wrong, attending endless internal meetings and generally manoeuvring inside the organisation. They point out that Mintzberg reported that the job of a manager has changed little in the last 100 years yet so many changes have taken place in the internal and external environments of the organisation and suggest that, therefore, managers must be doing the wrong things and that if the organisation is to thrive in the future there must be a change in the nature of what are regarded as managerial tasks. They go on to report that managers indulge in management activity largely for the benefit of managers and no one else. The problem is that the argument in favour of management is therefore totally circular: management is necessary and valuable because the corporation has been set up to require management.

Koch and Godden (1996) suggest that in the new organisations management might not be necessary or perhaps, less radically, that there will be a need for far fewer managers. They point out that small firms and partnerships have managed quite well without professional managers. Managers, they say, should aim to please customers by adding value to what the organisation does. They should leave new initiatives and changes to a few leaders in the organisation. Koch and Godden (1996) question whether managers are necessary to organise and supervise others, and suggest that research on self-managing teams or profit centres would seem to suggest that managers are largely superfluous for the purpose: 'the experience of virtually all businesses that have abolished a tier of supervisory task is that this improves performance on top of costs saved'. Do managers need to coordinate others and conduct administration? Process thinking, as exemplified in business process re-engineering, has shown ways out of such coordinating roles, they say: the team itself coordinates. Temporary task forces facilitate change and the computer can administer many tasks thousands of times better than managers. Similarly, modern technology can disseminate information and while financial control, often considered as a central feature of management activity, will still be necessary while corporations follow the current system, such control can be exercised with very few managers, as few as 20-30 people even in large organisations.

Koch and Godden (1996) conclude that most management is unnecessary and undesirable, except in the very largest and most complex organisations. As society shifts toward greater organisational democracy, companies will require that managers of the future spend more time in the leader role and in the external roles of figurehead, liaison, spokesman and negotiator. Koch and Godden (1996) suggest that managerial jobs might then be grouped into eight basic types[1]: contact man (for whom the liaison and figurehead roles are the most important); political manager (stressing the spokesman and negotiator roles); entrepreneur (entrepreneur and negotiator roles); insider (resource allocator role); real-time manager (disturbance handler role); team manager (leader role); expert (monitor and spokesman roles); and new manager (liaison and monitor roles).

While one may disagree with some aspects of their analysis, there can be little doubt that in the future many organisations will employ fewer managers than at present. The trend towards flatter management hierarchies and the elimination (or at least partial elimination) of tasks previously done by managers such as monitoring and supervising seems likely to result in a substantial reduction of the numbers of managers required.

BIBLIOGRAPHY

Anthony, Robert N. *Planning and Control Systems: a framework for analysis* (Cambridge, Mass.: Harvard University Press, 1965).

Gorry, G. Anthony and Scott Morton, Michael S. 'A Framework for Management Information Systems.' *Sloan Management Review,* Fall 1971, pp. 55-70.

Koch, Richard and Godden, Ian. *Managing Without Management: a post-management manifesto for business simplicity* (London: Nicholas Brealey, 1996).

McKinnon, Sharon M. and Bruns, William J. *The Information Mosaic* (Boston: Harvard Business School Press, 1992).

Mintzberg, Henry. *The Nature of Managerial Work* (New York: Harper and Row, 1973).

Mintzberg, Henry. 'The Manager's Job, Folklore or Fiction.' *Harvard Business Review,* July/August 1975, pp. 49-61.

Peters, T. *Thriving on Chaos* (London: Macmillan, 1989).

Peters, T. *Liberation Management* (London: Macmillan, 1992).

Pettinger, Richard. *Introduction to Organisational Behaviour* (Basingstoke: Macmillan, 1996).

Note

1   In brackets are the related roles delineated by Mintzberg (1973).

Chapter 3

Why do managers need information?

INTRODUCTION

A manager's need for information will depend on the decisions he/she needs to take in relation to his/her work, so it is appropriate to give some thought to the kinds of decisions managers need to make before going on to discuss his/her information needs.

THE RATIONAL MODEL OF MANAGERIAL BEHAVIOUR AND DECISION-MAKING

Most people think of managers as acting rationally and with purpose. Managers are believed to go through the stages of rational analysis and thinking before doing. The stereotypical manager, according to traditional thinking, is believed to work on one problem at a time, classify goals, assess the situation, formulate options, estimate likelihood of success, make a decision and then take action to implement that decision in the most efficient manner. The proponents of this so-called rational model assume that such managers make decisions based on complete rationality. According to this model the manager is believed to select the best course of action from all the available courses of action in order to maximise returns. Recent work, however, has shown that this model is not appropriate to describe managerial decision-making and more recently other researchers have proposed different models.

SIMON'S MODEL OF MANAGERIAL BEHAVIOUR AND DECISION-MAKING

Simon (1955) recognised that there is a large non-rational element to most people's thinking and behaviour. This is not merely related to the individual's intelligence but also depends upon, among other things, the environment in which the individual must take the decision. Simon suggested that it is rare that the environment in which the individual is working enables him/her to identify all the alternatives and then select the optimal alternatives: 'Most human decision-making, whether individual or organisational, is concerned with the discovery and selection of satisfactory alternatives; only in exceptional circumstances is it concerned with the discovery and selection of optimal alternatives' (Newell and Simon (1972)).

Simon (1960) proposed a new model to describe managerial decision making – that of 'administrative' man. He said that administrative man 'satisfices' rather than maximises; he looks for the course of action which is satisfactory or good enough rather than optimal. Simon (1960) explains that a decision-maker who satisfices is content with simplification, he/she takes into account only a few of the factors which might be deemed to be relevant to the decision. A manager who satisfices makes decisions without searching for all the possible alternatives, he/she does not search for the alternative that would yield an optimal solution but rather he/she searches for a satisfactory solution at this time. He/she has to decide whether to make a decision now and so choose from the alternatives currently available or to delay action and hope that a new alternative will be found at a later date which will yield a greater reward. The manager is seeking a feasible solution rather than an optimal solution. Simon (1960) explains that satisficing is caused by the following:

- the lack of information or the cost of additional information in terms of time, frustration or money;

- the inability of the decision-maker to process, analyse and use the information.

Simon (1960) went on to report that in most decisions there were so many variables involved that any attempt to reduce decision-making to that expected by the rational model was likely to be very crude and that there was no evidence that in complex situations human beings acted as predicted by the rational model. Only in specific areas, such those involving operational and management control tasks, where most activities are functional and routine, can much quantitative data be produced and so decisions can be made based on analysis of this data. Other decisions, such as strategic decisions, often require data which is often of a more behavioural nature and so is not subject to easy quantification; such data is often difficult to process, analyse and use.

Forrester (1961) explains that mathematical analysis can take care of the routine decision-making such as that required in operational and management control tasks, but it is of little value in helping the manager to seek out new business opportunities, predicting reactions to new products and company policies, negotiating new contracts, selecting employees or, indeed, handling the vast bulk of decision-making in which most managers engage in during most of their working day.

Structured and unstructured decisions[1]

Simon (1960) goes on to draw the distinction between programmed and non-programmed decisions. Such decisions are not mutually exclusive but form a continuum from highly programmed decisions at one end to highly unprogrammed at the other end. A decision is programmed to the extent that it is a routine decision for which there is already an established method with which it can be dealt. Such decisions are often regarded as standard operating procedures or clerical routine. A programmed decision is one which occurs repeatedly and the organisation has a clear procedure laid down to deal with it. Programmed decisions frequently occur at the operational level of the organisation. For instance, the organisation will have a clear procedure laid down to deal with decisions involved in sending out invoices or processing a customer order. A decision is unprogrammed to the extent that there is no routine or procedure to handle the problem, possibly because the situation has not occurred before or because it is very difficult problem. An example of an unprogrammed decision might be how to enter a new market or expand into a new product line. Of course, such an unprogrammed decision is likely to involve a series of smaller sub-decisions, many of which may be programmed, but for unprogrammed decisions the organisation must rely on its capacity for intelligent problem-solving and the ability of the individual managers to use their judgement, intuition and creativity rather than pre-existing methods of doing things.

Decision-making activity

In situations where fully programmed decision-making is not possible managers often go through several stages in making a decision:

- identifying situations which require a decision;
- problem definition – the essential details of the problem need to be identified, such as the environment, the people involved and the nature of the problem is explored and an attempt is made to understand the problem;
- information collection – information is collected within the constraints of time, cost and availability – few decisions are based on perfect information;
- generating alternative courses of action;
- evaluation of alternatives according to their expected outcomes – each solution may be assessed according to the desirability of its outcome, or the probability of its being successful. The relative advantages and disadvantages of each outcome may be weighed against each other and the solutions ranked accordingly;
- a solution is chosen;
- the solution is implemented;
- the results of the implemented solution are monitored and evaluated.

The process of making decisions is rarely straightforward and problems or new insights may generate a series of sub-problems each of which may require an iteration of the above sequence. Simon and Newell (1972) found that when a manager is faced with such a decision his/her response is to try to reduce the decision to a series of sub-decisions to which he/she can then apply the general purpose sets of procedures and routines which are used for other decisions. In short, the manager tries to reduce unstructured, unfamiliar problems to familiar structurable elements. He/she then tries to find a solution which will produce a satisficing solution rather than a maximal outcome.

The recognition that much of the important managerial decision-making is not of the simple progammable type which it was originally assumed to be has lead to more investigation of the type and nature of managerial decision-making.

NEW VIEWS OF DECISION-MAKING

Managers are frequently called upon to make non-progammed decisions; such decisions may be as part of the strategic planning process or in response to a change in the immediate environment. Mintzberg (1972) reports that each manager carries a great many models in his head; these will include models of the structure of the organisation, the industrial sector, competitors, products and services. These models are used to predict phenomena such as how a change in organisational structure will affect the workforce, how a change in price will affect the demand for a product. The manager also seems to have a set of loose plans which indicate the general direction in which the organisation should develop. The manager constantly updates these models and plans in the light of new information. Isenberg (1984) agrees; he says that managers have a portfolio of problems, issues and opportunities on which they work simultaneously. These problems are often interrelated and may compete for the manager's attention. Managers do not select one problem to solve at a time, nor do they have precise goals and objectives but rather overriding concerns. Sometimes the manager will discover that working on one problem will bring about the solution to another problem in the portfolio.

The particular problem that he/she chooses to work on at a particular time may be influenced by the manager's perception of how easy that problem is to solve at that time. Isenberg (1984) says there is evidence that managers tend not to think about a problem unless it is solvable; managers rely heavily on intuition to solve their problems. This 'gut feeling' is not irrational nor random, rather it is the result of extensive experience in both analysis and problem-solving, problem finding, problem definition and the generation of solutions. As Isenberg (1984) explains, 'senior managers often ignore the implied linear progression of the rational decision-making model and jump opportunistically from phase to phase allowing implementation concerns to affect the problem definition and perhaps even to limit the range of solutions generated.'

What is clear, however, from the work of writers such as Mintzberg and Isenberg, is that managers attend to strategy for only part of the day; it is not at the forefront of their consciousness all the time, they devote a lot of time to operational and management control tasks.

Manager's personal style

The way in which a manager makes a decision will depend to some extent on his or her personal style. Some managers make decisions very quickly, others find this less easy to do. Rowe (1984) reported that there are four basic decision-making styles:

- Directive style – managers with this style tend to be autocratic, enjoy power and maintain tight control over the area and people for which they are responsible. Their decision style is efficient and logical but they dislike ambiguity; they make decisions very quickly but the decisions are based on very little information; they consider few alternatives and focus on short range, internal factors.

- Analytical style – managers with an analytical style of decision-making have more tolerance for ambiguity than directive managers but they maintain control over the decision-making within the area for which they are responsible. Their decisions, however, are based on the collection of more information and they consider more alternatives than a directive manager and tend to be more analytical in their approach to the various phases of decision-making than directive managers; they enjoy problem-solving and strive to obtain maximum output.

- Conceptual style – conceptual managers are achievement-oriented, they have a broad outlook, they consider many alternatives and generate creative solutions focusing on long-term issues. They encourage others to participate in decisions and they negotiate well.

- Behavioural style – managers with this style are concerned with the development of people. They communicate easily, are persuasive and show empathy for those working for them. Their focus tends to be short or medium term and they tend to use limited data as their focus is on making decisions through people.

Group decisions and participation

Many organisations now encourage participative decision-making; indeed, in some organisations most of the decisions in the organisation are taken by groups of workers who will implement the decision.

There are limits to participative decision-making, however; it may, in some circumstances, produce lower quality decisions. It can, however, be very useful in encouraging a team-spirit, resolving disputes and difficulties, motivating staff and enabling greater acceptance of what might otherwise be unpalatable decisions among staff. At the managerial level many decisions are taken in groups and information processing in organisations often involves managers working together to develop a consensus about a problem. Different members of the group bring differing perceptions to the problem or differing interpretations of the same event, so the group must bridge this diversity and disagreement and converge on an acceptable solution or interpretation in the context of the organisation's goals.

Improving managerial decision-making

Gorry and Scott Morton (1971) say that most managers employ very primitive models of their environment and as a result the range of responses which they are able to generate is equally limited. They often use historical models when they anticipate the future; such models are often static, but the processes (the business environment) they purport to model are dynamic. This explicit recognition that much decision-making in organisations is less than optimal has resulted in new innovations to aid managerial decision-making. There is a belief that the approach to decision-making which comes naturally to most managers – working on a portfolio of problems at once – has much to recommend it. It enables the manager to seek a more multidimensional solution without the constraints of defined goals and objectives.

There has been a recognition that it is frequently not the lack of information which hampers managerial decision-making, but rather the inability of the manager to process the information, so developments in technology such as decision support tools have helped to some extent.

Most managers recognise that their capacity for decision-making may be inhibited and they may employ new ways to overcome the limitations this may impose. For instance, they may be aware that it is easy to fall into habitual ways of doing things and they actively seek out a wide variety of reading material or new experiences which expose them to differing modes of thinking. They may train themselves to pay particular attention to their own feelings of surprise when something novel happens to see what they can learn from that situation, whereas in the past they might have dismissed such novelty as a mere anomaly. Another method of preventing habitual modes of thinking and operating is to instigate a course of action to see what can be learnt from it. For instance, a chief executive might buy a company to learn more about how it does business.

Clearly the rational model of decision-making has been largely superseded by a more holistic and pragmatic approach to managerial decision making; this has implications for some of the traditional assumptions about information use, and hence provision within the organisation, and it is the use of information by the decision-maker that is now considered.

PROBLEMS WITH MANAGERIAL INFORMATION USE

Introduction

It seems reasonable to suppose that when a manager (or, indeed, any other person) is faced with a decision, he/she will require any information which might be perceived to be relevant. Yet both research and anecdotal evidence indicate that this frequently does not happen. This finding clearly has implications for the providers of information such as libraries and information units and for those who design and implement the mechanisms by which such information is delivered. It is appropriate, therefore, to spend some time trying to discover why managers (and indeed other users) behave in this seemingly irrational way. What are the factors which prevent managers from using information? Mintzberg (1975) suggests there are three impediments to the use of information for management/tactical control and these may also to be applicable to the use of information required for the performance of other managerial tasks such as operational control and strategy formulation:

- organisational dysfunction,
- problems with the information itself,
- the manager's cognitive limitations.

A manager's ability to use the information available seems to be determined by the interplay of all these factors, though some will obviously be more important than others at different times and in different environments and in the performance of differing managerial roles. The problems of information use caused by organisational dysfunction are dealt with in chapter 1, while the problems caused by the information itself can be found in chapter 5. This section considers cognitive limitations experienced by a manager and the consequences for decision-making.

Cognitive limitations to the use of information

A cognitive limitation is an inability to process further relevant information: 'the capacity of the human mind for formulating and solving complex problems is very small compared with the size of the problems whose solution is required for objectively rational behaviour in the real world – or even for a reasonable approximation to such objective reality' (Simon (1957).

Several of these limitations will be familiar to most people:

- too much information,
- too little time,
- stress and fatigue,
- pressure of other demands.

Other factors, while less obvious may, nevertheless, severely restrict a manager's ability to process information:

- tendency of brain to filter information in line with predetermined patterns and beliefs;
- discomfiture and threat felt when information disagrees with current belief;
- lack of information literacy resulting in an inability to understand what might constitute relevant information.

Processing ability of managers

For many organisations and those who work in them change is the norm, yet many people are uncomfortable with change and may even seek to avoid it where possible. It is not difficult to understand why those charged with the task of managing the organisation and improving its competitive position might feel threatened and uncomfortable when their working environment is in almost constant flux. Change may be perceived as threatening and, as Straw, Sandelands and Dutton

(1981) point out, there is often a tendency for people to behave rigidly in such situations. Such perceptions of threat may often result in a restriction of information collection and processing and possibly in a reduction in the number of sources investigated, which will restrict the information available on which to base strategic decisions, thus possibly prejudicing the future of the organisation.

It is not only the perception of threat which may cause managers (and indeed many other people) to restrict their information collection – managers tend to expose themselves to ideas that are in accordance with their current ideas and beliefs – they read the same paper, see the same people and as a consequence their own perceptions and ideas about the world are constantly reinforced rather than challenged. It is not surprising, therefore, that information which contradicts their view of the world may be viewed with scepticism. Indeed, so great might be their suspicion of such information that they might ignore it altogether. As Mintzberg (1975) and Wilson and Walsh (1995) explain, people have a tendency to filter out information which does not conform to existing beliefs, experience, values and attitudes. We all have our own concepts and models about how the world is; these have been built up over our lifetimes and we use them to make predictions about the world, altering them gradually as our predictions prove more or less correct. With processes such as strategic planning, however, managers may be required to question the very nature of the businesses they are in, so it might not even be obvious what questions need to be asked, let alone what answers are required, so the collection of information for such a task is likely to be difficult. It is not surprising, therefore, that information which is sought for strategic planning might not initially be recognised as useful. Firstly, it might not fit in with existing beliefs about the current state and future of the organisation; the information received may go completely against existing ideas about the state of the organisation, its environment and its future prospects. Secondly, people have a tendency to consider new problems in terms of previous ones, so it might be difficult to recognise the relevance of some information without a clear issue for which it might be regarded as important. As a result, managers may filter out potentially relevant information. All of these problems are compounded by the curious finding by Radecki and Jackard (1995) that the more important a topic is perceived to be, the more likely a person is to regard him/ herself as knowledgeable about it (and hence the less likely he/she is to seek further information about it).

Modern organisations are often very stressful places in which to work and research indicates that stress (perhaps brought on by change or simply the pressures of work and domestic life) may add a further dimension to the problems of information processing. Stress inhibits a subject's ability to perform tasks and this may also inhibit the ability to make decisions about the relevance of information. Reuters (1996) survey revealed that 41% of managers believe that their workplace is stressful and 56% believe that it will become more stressful in the future.

Information overload

There is no universally agreed definition of information overload – it can mean several things, such as having more relevant information than one can assimilate. It might mean being burdened with a large supply of unsolicited information, some of which may be relevant. In every case, however, there is an implication that the overabundance of information forces the manager to spend more time and energy processing the information than he/she might wish to.

It is tempting to ask why managers get themselves into the position in which they appear to be overwhelmed by information. Of all the people working in the organisation, they are in the best position to control their working environment and hence their information load. It is helpful, therefore, to consider why they choose to have so much information available even if they then complain about the amount. There are, it seems seven main reasons why organisations and individuals collect an overabundance of information:

- Western tradition – As Feldman and March (1981) point out, the western world prides itself on being a rational culture and the use of information symbolises a commitment to rational choice. The collection of information indicates that one is committed to rationalism and is perceived as indicating competence and this implies better decision-making.

- Unsolicited information – many managers do not even have to actively seek out information – it just arrives. Unsolicited information far outweighs requested information, with 33% of managers reporting that they receive 'enormous amounts' of unsolicited information, according to Reuters (1996). The problem of unsolicited information is exacerbated by the huge improvements in information and communication technologies (ICTs) which enable lengthy reports to be distributed to a wide audience with no extra effort on the part of the author, and thus they provide access to an ever increasing amount of information. As organisations increase their use of Management Information Systems (MIS), the task of data reduction becomes more difficult. Wildavsky (1983) reports that MIS reduce the chance that collectable data might remain uncollected, but the question of whether it should be collected often goes unasked. 80% of managers believe that the reason for information overload is because external and internal communications are increasing rapidly, according to Reuters (1996).

- Information checking – Wildavsky (1983) reports that there seems to be a belief that the collection of more information will enable one to check the information that one already has; unfortunately, very frequently the opposite happens. The collection of yet more information only serves to muddy the waters and introduce more variables and uncertainty which then necessitates the collection of more information to determine the information on which to base the decision.

- Justifying decisions – the production of large amounts of information can be used to demonstrate that a decision must be correct because it has been based on such a large quantity of information. Should the decision subsequently prove to be incorrect, then the assemblage of a vast amount of information can be used to prove to peers that one tried one's best. Information enables one to justify one's position. In the Reuters (1996) survey, 32% of managers think that colleagues are forced to collect information to justify their position.

- Just-in-case – there is also an element of 'just-in-case' to the collection of vast amounts of information. In the current business environment it is often difficult to determine what is going to happen next and the collection of information seems to provide a kind of reassurance to some people that there is nothing nasty 'lurking in the woodshed'. As Ackoff (1967) suggests, in order for a manager to know what information he needs, he must know all the decisions which he will need to make both now and in the future and to have an adequate model of each of them. This is clearly impossible. From this perspective, therefore, it may make sense to collect as much information as possible and from as broad a spectrum as possible.

- Sorting out the variables – even when a manager is aware of the nature of the decisions which will need to be taken in the future it is often difficult to be precise about what information is required to make those decisions. So a manager who does not understand the phenomenon about which he has to make a decision is likely to play it safe and ask for everything. By asking for everything, however, there is even less time to assimilate and interpret the available information.

- Keeping-up-with colleagues – some people collect information because they know that their colleagues are collecting information and they cannot afford to be left behind or shown up as being less well informed than others.

Five out of the seven reasons for managerial overload given above are based on fear, of one kind or another, and this fear may lead to stress. This is important since in a recent Reuters (1996) survey 70% of managers reported that they suffer stress at some time or other as a result of information overload. Of more concern is that 62% say that their personal relationships suffer because of the volume of information. 49% feel that they are quite often or very often unable to deal with the volume of information they receive and 43% believe that important decisions are delayed and their ability to make decisions is affected as a result of too much information. Too much information is clearly contributing to personal stress and anxiety; we all need to process information in order to perform our jobs yet we are in danger of being overwhelmed by the amount of potentially useful information. The burden of keeping up-to-date seems to be taking its toll on our health and quality of life.

The effects of information overload pose worrying dilemmas for organisations in addition to individuals. Too much information can affect the performance of managers and hence of organisations in several ways, both direct and indirect:

- The load of information causes stress which affects performance. Clearly not all this stress is caused by information overload but it appears to add to the problem. Stress may cause hyper-arousal which in turn adversely affects the manager's ability to make decisions.

- There is evidence to suggest that too much information leads to individual underperformance and that behaviour may become dysfunctional. Jacoby (1974) has demonstrated that there are finite limits to the ability of human beings to assimilate and process information during a given unit of time. When these limits are exceeded behaviour becomes confused and dysfunctional. Iselin (1989) has demonstrated that, in a business context, an over-abundance of information increases decision time; too much information decreases the ability to select the relevant information and thus increases the distraction of irrelevant information. This may then become a vicious circle.

- The collection and interpretation of the information may get in the way of performance of main job responsibilities.

- Decision making may be further prejudiced by the mechanisms which individuals adopt to cope with an overabundance of information. Miller (1962), Katz and Kahn (1966) and Weick (1970) refer to 'adjustment processes' which are routinely adopted; these include:

    - failure to process some information – this may take the form of inability to locate the required information because of sheer volume;

    - faulty processing of information – which may take the form of overlooking what is most critical among relevant data;

    - queuing or catching up rather then keeping up – adding incoming information to a 'to be read' pile which results in a backlog;

    - filtering or the systematic omission of certain categories of information;

    - approximation – cutting categories of information because there is no time in which to deal with the information;

    - escape or withdrawal from the information situation altogether;

    - redefining the situation, thus changing the quantity of or the relevance of the information required.

All of the above may have serious consequences for decision-making.

Recognition of a problem of information overload is often the first step to alleviating it but the remedies sought may cause further problems within the organisation:

- Reduction of the amount of information – superficially an attractive and, indeed, obvious solution, reduction of the total amount of information is rarely a satisfactory solution as it may create as

many problems as it solves. Steps taken to reduce the information load may include a reduction of environmental scanning.
Such measures, however, may result in inadequate information
about the external world which may in turn cause the organisation to focus too narrowly on operational goals with serious
consequences for its long-term success.

- The organisation may choose to limit the channels by which information is disseminated and possibly introduce a policy that
information is distributed on a 'need-to-know' basis. Problems
arise in this situation because it is rare that everyone in the organisation knows what everyone else needs to know and such a
solution needs to be thought out carefully.

- Similarly, there are problems when the organisation introduces
more vertical differentiation to encourage information filtering
since in most modern organisations a large number of management levels is rarely desirable and the introduction of horizontal
differentiation such as the creation of information and research
units and strategic business units, as we have seen, may create a
further set of problems.

Lack of information literacy

Many senior managers who are now in the position of decision-makers in organisations were educated when the use of information
technology in organisations was in its infancy. Kanter (1996) points out
that some managers still perceive the technology as a means to automate functions such as accounting and production and, while they may
have attained computer literacy and are familiar with word proces-
sors, spreadsheets, databases, email and other software packages, they
have yet to attain information literacy. Information literacy is a much
wider concept than computer literacy; it implies an appreciation of
technology as an enabler, rather than as a simple tool with which to
automate functions. The attainment of information literacy implies an
understanding that information is a valuable competitive resource and
should be managed and used as such. It implies that the manager un-
derstands that it is the information and business needs of the
organisation that must determine the technology rather than vice versa,
and that the organisation's information technology must be aligned
with its corporate strategy rather then dictating that strategy. An information literate manager will ensure that the organisation's information
architecture is designed so that the organisation will be in a position
to take advantage of organisational and indeed global connectivity,
and that the organisation is in a position to take advantage of any new
appropriate technologies.

Information literacy may occur as a direct result of training of managers or possibly of external consultation. It may occur as a result of a
business process re-engineering exercise or the introduction of a new
technology platform such as datawarehousing.

It is seems reasonably clear, however, that most businesses that wish to thrive in the next century must aspire to become more information- and knowledge-based. Such organisations must, therefore, devise ways by which appropriate information can be collected, stored and disseminated and they must find ways in which organisational knowledge can be leveraged and the first step for many organisations must be to determine their information needs.

WHAT ARE THE INFORMATION NEEDS OF MANAGERS?

Introduction

As we have seen, in many business situations it is almost impossible to obtain every bit of relevant information for decision-making even if the manager requires this, which is frequently not the case. Taylor (1986) says that the possession of 70% of available information is considered high in most decision-making situations. Indeed, in some situations (excluding many operational and management control situations) it may be impossible to provide perfect information, particularly as the information itself may be ambiguous and even contradictory. Even when managers recognise that their decision requires additional information they find it difficult to identify their needs. Many managers seem unable to explain their needs and there seem to be several reasons for this:

- they are unaware of what information is available;
- they do not understand how such information can be used;
- they are unaware of the delivery method options.

As a consequence, those charged with the provision of information within the organisation, such as the staff of the library and information unit and the builders of information systems, often design their systems based on assumptions about the kinds of information which the managers of the organisations in question will require; they make expensive decisions about information provision based on discussions and interviews with the relevant managers but there are considerable dangers with this method. It assumes that:

- managers are aware of what information is available from both internal and external sources (which they frequently are not);
- managers are aware of what decisions they will need to take both now and in the future (which is highly unrealistic);
- the information required to support their decisions and their work is available (which it frequently is not);
- if the information was available then the manager would be able to use it (which may or may not be true);
- if relevant information is available then it will affect their decision-making (which may or may not be true).

As we have seen, most managers have an idea of some of the decisions that they need to make; Mintzberg (1972) suggests that managers seem to carry models and plans around in their heads which can be used to predict phenomena such as how an increase in costs of raw materials will affect price or how a change in employment legislation will affect recruitment. These models and plans are constantly updated as new information is received. New information may also trigger activity such as searching for a business opportunity (in his role as entrepreneur) or it may cause the manager to initiate crisis handling measures.

Clearly, as Mintzberg (1972) suggests, managers who carry round models and plans must already have internal personal information databases of considerable size and complexity if decisions are to be made effectively. There is little research about how information-seeking habits of managers increase their information stores but research carried out among members of the scientific community may help to throw some light on why managers need information. The work of Wilson and Walsh (1995) and Weigts et al (reported in Wilson and Walsh (1995)) suggest that scientists have:

- a need for new information,
- a need to elucidate information held,
- a need to confirm information held,
- a need to elucidate and confirm beliefs and values.

New information may be required to build up the manager's understanding of the subject and to further develop and refine the internal models of that subject. A manager who does not understand a phenomenon is, as we have seen, likely to seek all the information he/she can obtain. As a recent Reuters survey (1996) indicated, managers who perceive uncertainty in their markets require a lot of information and expect their information requirements to increase in the future.

Managerial roles and their information requirements

Taylor (1986) points out that there has been in huge increase in the volume of information which may be perceived as relevant to business and this has altered the information environment within which managers must work. There is information available from internal information systems or from external sources and, as Taylor (1986) goes on to explain, managers use this information to clarify their options or identify alternative courses of action and, of course, they are seeking information which might alert them to a business opportunity.

However, whatever the role or indeed the task, information will almost certainly be vital to its successful performance. The precise type and nature of the information required, however, will differ depending on which role or task is currently being performed. It is, therefore, of interest to consider managerial information requirements within this context.

Information needs for operational tasks

Operational tasks are performed by virtually all managers at all levels of the organisation at some time during their working week. As shown above, the precise nature of their operational tasks will, however, depend on a number of factors including seniority and the sector of industry in which they work. Operational tasks can usually be defined in functional terms and include divisions such as production, marketing and sales. Managers involved in operational tasks require information which is usually of the form 'How many items were produced today?', 'How many items did we sell today?', 'How much coal did we use today?', 'How many people were absent today?'.

Those responsible for operational tasks are concerned about costs and productivity of the raw materials they employ and reports of events such as downtime, output and raw material usage and scrap are vital to the efficient running of the traditional factory. McKinnon and Bruns (1992) say that in the performance of their operational tasks managers often require information about the quality of production and of the raw materials; this includes obvious indicators such as scrap rates, information on routine maintenance, unplanned breakdowns, failures and production problems. The latter gets much attention because unanticipated problems must be solved to ensure that planned production can be completed. Raw materials and production capacity must be used in the most efficient and cost-effective manner possible; production problems can be very expensive and will often have an impact on other functional departments such as sales and distribution, so such information is important for the successful completion of operational tasks.

The information provided for the management of operations is used to monitor current progress and to determine scheduling of future events and, as McKinnon and Bruns (1992) point out, the physical nature of operational tasks such as production, sales and logistical processes often leads to the collection of operational information using direct observation of the process or reports of such observation. Indeed, there is much at the operational level which can be observed, counted and reported on – materials arrive and are processed, goods are shipped. It is, therefore, a relatively simple task for managers or others to whom the task has been delegated to observe directly what happens and then compare this with what was expected or what must be done to achieve financial results that will satisfy or better established targets. Similarly, information at the operational level in marketing and sales is largely obtained by direct observation; for instance, the number of orders placed during a specific time span. The amount of money generated by such orders is also of interest but usually in the longer term; it is the immediacy of orders placed which is of particular interest at the operational stage, while the pattern of orders may give preliminary indications of possible changes in market demand. Sales information is also closely linked to inventory for many organisations and so inventory information is also very important to sales departments and again such information is amenable to direct observation, often a simple count.

McKinnon and Bruns (1992) point out, however, that in marketing departments some information required for operational tasks may be more difficult to obtain. The success or otherwise of a marketing campaign might be measured by the increase in sales over the corresponding period in the previous year, though this is by no means infallible as there may be several other variables which might account for the increase. Marketing departments are also interested in maintaining and improving good customer relationships since satisfied customers are a prime source of new orders. However, information about customer satisfaction is usually difficult to collect. One measure of customer satisfaction might be the number of customer complaints; but it would not be wise to rely on the number of complaints received by the organisation since some customers may not complain directly but register their dissatisfaction by switching to an alternative supplier. Some measure of levels of customer satisfaction may be gleaned by talking directly to the customer at events such as trade fairs and from the sales force as they visit customers on their own premises. Less direct methods may also include a measure of the requests for maintenance and technical backup or support – should these suddenly increase then this should alert the organisation to problems – as might a lengthening of delivery times for both the product and its spare parts. Such information is important and marketing managers are desperate for such information on a day-to-day basis.

Much of the information required for operational tasks is quantitative, though, as we have seen, this is not always true in functions such as marketing. To be useful, however, operational information must be accurate, detailed, highly structured, well-defined and narrow in scope. Such information is often produced directly as a by-product of the operational process itself, often in real-time or very soon after the event. For instance, many manufacturing processes provide data concerning how much of each raw material is currently being consumed and the number of items produced in a given period, and in sales departments orders are produced as a direct result of the act of selling. The information provided for these operational purposes is also frequently used as the raw data which informs those responsible for the managerial control/tactical tasks, though in manipulated form.

Information needs for managerial control/tactical tasks
Information for management control/tactical tasks is required to enable the manager to ensure that the business is progressing satisfactorily towards the achievement of its aims and objectives. There are likely to be aims and objectives for each function or business activity cluster in the organisation. Many organisations set specific targets for each operation or business cluster which will ensure that the overall aims and objectives of the business will be met. Such targets may take the form of, for instance, a 10% increase in sales over the previous year or a decrease in cost of production of 5% over the previous quarter. Infor-

mation for management control/tactical tasks is obtained from largely internal sources and often takes the form of an aggregation of the raw data which is produced as a by-product of the operational processes discussed above. Such aggregation may be weekly or monthly summaries of the operations or processes for which the manager is responsible and may include relevant financial information about the costs of inputs and outputs. Often such information merely confirms that the operations and processes are proceeding in a way which has been anticipated and thus confirms that the organisation is on target to achieve its overall aims and objectives; occasionally, however, the information will be at variance with what is expected or desired and when such anomalies occur they may indicate that there is a problem which must be attended to immediately to ensure that the targets are met. In short, management control/tactical information enables the manager to manage by exception – to concentrate on what is going wrong rather than needing to pay attention to all aspects of the business operation or process.

The specific types of information sought for the purpose of management / tactical control will depend to a large extent on the functions or process for which the manager is responsible, but may include information about the productivity of the workforce, use of raw materials and equipment and benchmarking against other similar operations both within the organisation and against the best in the sector. It may also include information about core competencies such as innovations measurement and information concerning the allocation of scarce resources such as capital and people.

Information needs for strategic tasks

Strategy formulation is the management task which determines the future direction of the organisation and as such it involves an attempt to predict the future not only of the organisation but also of the environment in which the organisation will conduct its business. Many organisations are now guided by the work of Michael Porter during their strategic planning and recognise that effective strategy must take into account not only the actions of direct rivals but also the role of suppliers and the actions of customers and so they seek to identify not only obvious competing products but those alternative products which may satisfy the same customer needs as their own products. During the strategic planning process organisations should also consider the prospects of new entrants to their market. For instance, it has been suggested that such a threat occasioned the entrance of some of the UK retail food supermarkets onto the Internet. The companies in this sector believed that it was in their own long-term strategic interests to provide goods and services on the Internet because such interests would be damaged if some other organisation, possibly as yet unknown, began to offer food and related goods and services on the Internet. Such a competitor would pose a very serious threat to existing retail food companies since it might take away a substantial part of their market by undercutting them. This could be achieved because such a competitor need not carry the costs of the substantial investment in prime site real estate which characterises much of the current sector but, rather, could operate directly from warehouses to which the retail customer has no access. The strategic information which resulted in a move onto the Internet might have included details of the buying habits of customers and new delivery mechanisms, but of equal importance would be information about the new technologies which have changed market conditions by removing an important entry barrier to the market – that of the requirement for retail space.

As McGee and Prusak (1992) point out, by forcing those involved to be more specific about their strategic needs the Porter model should also help managers to define the information they require. The model forces them to consider alternative products, products which might emerge to satisfy customer expectations, and to consider the possibility of new entrants into their markets. As a consequence the use of the model usually increases the demand for information since it increases the number of variables that need to be considered by those involved in strategy formulation. However, the huge increase in the number of variables coupled with the vast increase in the number of information sources and media may make the provision of information for strategic planning more rather then less difficult than previously. Aguilar (1967) suggests that, unlike the information required for operational and management control/tactical tasks, no information is inherently strategic. Any information may be regarded as strategic to the extent that it is used as part of the strategic planning process or to provide a business opportunity. As such, the information which those involved in strategy formulation will perceive that they require will depend on their ability to isolate those variables which will determine the future of the organisation.

Information required for strategic planning also differs in other ways from the information provided for other management tasks. It is often loosely structured, it need not be completely accurate, it should be predictive rather than historical – it may take the form of trends – and it is likely to be qualitative rather than quantitative.

Performance and information use

Introduction
Information is intangible and it is often very difficult to measure the contribution which it makes to the success or otherwise to the organisation as a whole, let alone to the performance of individual managers. However, as so many organisations need to demonstrate their efficient use of resources and information is one of their most important resources, it is likely that, in the future, organisations will attempt to demonstrate the effect which the use of information has on the performance of the organisation as a whole and the individual manager in particular. Care needs to be taken to disentangle several problems to obtain a clearer understanding of the problem of measuring the contribution made by information:

- Is it the use of information technology or the use of information which has improved performance? In many organisations technology has had profound effect on the form, manipulability and delivery of information products. Thus, for instance, many organisations have always made trade and related information available in the form of manuals and handbooks but technology has made access to, and use of, such information very much easier and has enabled the information to be updated more quickly and improved the portability of the information. Similarly, KPMG (1990) suggest that corporate failure or poor performance is often caused by the failure of the corporate information systems to inform directors about adverse changes in the environment.

- Even where potentially useful information is available the manager/organisation might not be able to use it. Many managers find it very difficult to state what information would be useful to them for strategic tasks, though, as we have seen, this is less of a problem for operational and management/tactical control tasks.

Difficulties of measuring the usefulness of information

It should, therefore, be clear that one is unlikely to be able to say in many situations that the use of information has improved organisational performance by a specific percentage and it follows, therefore, that it is equally difficult to measure the improvements caused by information to the performance of individual managers. Indeed, few organisations have even made an attempt to measure it. Aguilar (1967) reports that two out of the 41 companies he surveyed had tried to evaluate the success or otherwise of their scanning activities. They began with an appraisal of the relative success of the decision and then made an attempt to determine the critical information which by its presence or absence or its accuracy or inaccuracy appeared to contribute to the success or failure of the decision. Following these steps consideration was given to why the critical information was or was not obtained and steps taken to ensure a good outcome in future. While to some extent valid, this method is not foolproof – it may be difficult to determine the success or otherwise of a decision even with the benefit of hindsight.

In some organisations the problem of measuring the contribution made by information has a very important consequence – in times of recession the facilities providing information are often the first to be cut since they may be perceived as not making a contribution. This may have severe unforeseen consequences for the organisation. Obviously there are some organisations to which one can point where the possession (or lack) of information has determined the future of the organisation. Similarly the provision of a commissioned report from management consultants may have the effect of alerting the organisation to problems ahead and hence enabling it to avoid them. But in the general everyday work of the organisation and individual it is difficult to measure the contribution made by information.

Evidence of improved performance

Many factors will influence the performance of a company, such as the economic climate, changing trading conditions, competitive influences and technical or scientific developments, in addition to its own performance. Many organisations, however, are keen to gauge their own performance and many managers and writers on management rely on financial criteria to assess the success or otherwise of the enterprise. It is argued that such measures are useful because only companies which are financially sound will be able to grow. Such measures have the advantage that they are relatively easy to calculate and, as they are quantitative, they can be used to assess performance in comparison with organisational performance in previous years and against competitors.

In recent years, however, there has been some criticism of the use of financial measures to determine performance – they are regarded as rather crude. Abell (1995) points out that while such methods might indicate current success, few companies remain as top performers in terms of sales and growth over a long period. Consequently, new measures of success have been devised; these include customer satisfaction, quality, employee morale, innovation, competitiveness, stockholder returns and job creation.

Researchers have used both empirical methods and case studies to asses the performance of a company and relate it to the effective use of information and information systems. Broadbent (quoted in Abell (1995)) used a critical success factor methodology to demonstrate the value of information services to managers by linking information use to organisational outcomes. Prusak (quoted in Abell (1995)), in a survey of top Japanese companies, showed that they spend much time collecting, processing and disseminating business intelligence. He described them as having 'a preoccupation with the actions of their competitors' and suggests that it is this use of information which helps to maintain their competitive position.

In a case study of the US pharmaceutical industry in 1992, Koenig (quoted in Abell (1995)) tried to calculate the benefits of information on productivity which he defined as the number of new drugs per dollar of research budget. He found that in that in comparison with the four least productive companies the four most productive companies showed:

- more openness to information;
- less interest in protecting their proprietary information;
- more development of information systems;
- more use of information;
- greater technical and subject specialisation of the information services staff within the organisation.

While offering some evidence that information does make a contribution to the success or otherwise of the enterprise, the difficulty of isolating the contribution made by information alone is amply demonstrated. It might be more helpful, therefore, to discuss the contribution which a culture of information within the organisation can make to the success of the enterprise rather than attempt to calculate the benefits of information in isolation.

Importance of the development of an information culture

The culture of a company will depend on its organisation and structure and will permeate all aspects of the business. The culture will be reflected in the values of the organisation, its patterns of behaviour and the way in which members of the organisation interact with each other and the external world. It is generally believed that the culture of an organisation can have a considerable impact on an organisation's long-term economic performance.

An information culture is part of the corporate culture and, in turn, influences that corporate culture. Ginman (1988) defines an information culture as one in which the 'transformation of intellectual resources is maintained alongside the transformation of material resources. The primary resources for this type of transformation are varying kinds of knowledge and information'.

Ginman (1988) went on to say that an information culture depended on the degree of interest an organisation displayed in information and its attitude to factors in the external company environment, i.e. interest in the kind of information which might be located as a result of environmental scanning. Ginman (1988) interviewed 39 Chief Executive Officers and asked questions about their use of internal and external information, their attitude to information and quantity of information which they used. Ginman (1988) also looked at the company to determine size, age, level of research, know-how and knowledge as well as the internal and external communication and the development phase, life cycle and culture of the companies. Ginman's work showed that in an organisation where there is substantial market growth and an increased market share there is an intense interest in information. Risks are high and competition is keen in such organisations; there is fast feedback to the organisation about the success or otherwise of the product and about competitors, much of which is fed back into strategies. As a consequence the whole company is very aware of the importance of information collection and dissemination. Ginman demonstrated that the Chief Executive Officers of such companies try to create an environment where information flows freely through the company and he/she actively encourages communication maintaining a broad information and reading profile himself. Ginman also showed that in organisations which have a declining market share there was a hostile attitude to information.

Similarly, Daft, Sormunen and Parks (1988) also found that Chief Executive Officers in high performing companies made more and better use of information – they concentrated on how Chief Executive Officers reacted to perceived strategic uncertainty. Daft, Sormunen and Parks (1988) found that Chief Executive Officers in high performing companies scanned more frequently and more broadly in response to strategic uncertainty, though all increased their scanning in response to such uncertainty. Chief Executive Officers in higher performing companies were shown to focus their scanning more directly in those sectors perceived to be problematic, such as customer, economic, competitor, technological, regulatory, and sociocultural sectors. In short, their scanning behaviour was not fixed but varied with perceived uncertainty. In lower performing firms scanning behaviour did not vary with strategic uncertainty to the same degree. The actions of the Chief Executive Officer do not, of course, prove that the success of the company is due to the broader but more focused scanning. It may be that the very success of the company enables a different pattern of scanning, as Daft, Sormunen and Parks (1988) point out. It may be that higher performing firms have 'slack' in the system which means that the Chief Executive Officers can devote more of their time in the search for opportunities and problems, while Chief Executive Officers of lower performing companies are required to spend more of their time 'fire-fighting' and so there is less time for scanning. It is tempting, however, to assume that it is the scanning pattern adopted by the Chief Executive Officer which results in the success for the company. Chief Executive Officers from high performing companies do not seem to form impressions based on narrow information – their broader scanning even of what might be thought of initially as less relevant sectors such as sociocultural sectors, provides information about trends, opportunities, problems and other issues on which reflective decisions can be made. It may be, therefore, that the very success of scanning may become self-reinforcing and improved performance then provides the slack in the system which provides the opportunity for more and broader scanning.

There is evidence, as shown above, that many organisations are now recognising the importance of information (as opposed to information technology); indeed, many now regard it as a strategic resource, and this often leads to the development of an information culture in many organisations. Abell (1994) has shown that information has become a central issue for many firms, though it is often the management of information rather than the identification of useful information which they perceive as important. Owens and Wilson (1997) found that among the high performing companies which they surveyed a majority felt that their knowledge-base resided in the accumulated knowledge of their staff. So it seems that with increased awareness of the importance of information there is beginning to be a perception that information needs to be managed. All of which implies that organisations are now recognising that information does contribute to the success of the organisation even if its contribution is often difficult to measure.

It is clear that that a highly developed information culture correlates positively with successful business performance. Indeed, Ginman (1988) suggests that a company's attitude to information is closely connected with other significant organisational activities such as attitude and business culture and its stage in the life cycle, all of which are indicative of the success or otherwise of the organisation itself. A strong information culture seems to be indicative of a successful organisation; an organisation in which information resources are planned for and managed as meticulously as the material resources by which the organisation makes its living. It also implies considerable commitment from all members of the organisation including those at the top of the organisation.

So, there is increasing evidence that organisations recognise the importance of information and its management; however, as we have seen there is often considerable confusion about the information which will be useful for the organisation and its members and it is this subject which is now considered.

Methodologies for discovering information needs

Introduction

Those charged with the responsibility for the provision of information in organisations usually include computer professionals and information specialists. An organisation may also contain appropriately staffed Special Business Units and Research and Development Units. Both the computing and information professions have been keen to establish formal ways in which the information needs of managers may be determined – simply asking the relevant managers has not proved satisfactory for several reasons. In spite of the best efforts of management educators, managers still often find it difficult to determine what information they need, particularly at the strategic level, nor do they know what information is available or the many different ways it can be delivered to them.

The diverse nature of the information and its media and the differing nature of the tasks for which the information is required have frequently resulted in adverse criticism of the information-providing functions in many organisations and this in turn has led to the development of more systematic methods of determining such needs by both the computing and the information profession. The latter concentrated on the development of an information needs analysis which, while a useful tool, may be regarded as rather inward looking since its primary purpose is to ensure that the unit itself can provide for the information needs of the organisation. The computing and information systems professions have developed several methods for determining the information needs of management, culminating in the critical success factors approach, variations of which are still relied on today. Even this method, however, is only likely to be appropriate for the determination of information needs at the management control/tactical rather than the strategic level.

The use of several of the methodologies may be more successful than the use of one. However, given the diverse nature of information requirements, particularly at the strategic level, it is highly unlikely that any method or mix of methods will satisfy the need for information for all tasks in the organisation, though the use of such a method might help to determine information needs at the control/tactical and operational levels.

Information needs analysis

An information needs analysis is used principally by the library and information professions; it enables them to:

- identify the gap between their current provision of information resources and the level of service which the organisation will require in the future,

- forecast the nature of that future need (it may also include the forecast of the future delivery mechanisms),

- plan well in advance of the actual need and should ensure that there are systems, procedures and policies in place to meet the demand.

Methods used in analyzing information needs include customer surveys, currently available data about the organisation such as that found in the strategic plan, organisational statistics, forecasts and trends. Use also may be made of management techniques such as **S**trengths, **W**eaknesses, **O**pportunities and **T**hreats analyses to determine the capacity of the service to cope with the additional demands.

Key indicators

Rockart (1979) explains that in this method the key indicators of the health of the business are identified and detailed information is collected on each of these. This method relies heavily on financial information and the aim is to identify those areas where performance differs from planned performance. This method will be familiar as standard management information to many managers. There are problems with this method, however – it can result in a lot of data and, as will be demonstrated, the usefulness of such data often depends on the nature of its presentation and may not be targeted to the needs of specific managers.

Business Systems Planning (BSP)

This system was developed by IBM. Rockart (1979) reports that it arose out of the need to provide valuable information to managers rather than information which arises as a by-product of operational systems, which was what happened previously. A large number of managers are interviewed about their information needs, with the intention of gathering information about their work, responsibilities, objectives and decisions. The aim is to develop as complete an overall picture of the business as possible, together with an indication of the information which is necessary to manage the business and the existing information systems which currently provide this information. Information requirements are derived from the object system in a top-down fashion by starting with business objectives and then defining the processes. Business processes are used as the basis for data collection and analysis. A lot of time and money is devoted to the process and results in a vast amount of information together with tools with which to analyse it. The ultimate aim is often to build a total corporate information system which will cater for the information needs of the managers. Often, however, this method results in a system which is cumbersome and not tailored to the specific needs of any particular manager.

Critical Success Factors (CSFs)

This method is probably the most used and referred to in the literature. Popularised by Rockart (1979), this method is similar to the key success factors method given above in that it aims to identify those areas which are critical for the success of the business and identify that information which is needed to measure that success. As such, it is concerned with information which is needed to control, monitor and improve existing areas of business. Unlike the key indicator method and BSP methods, however, it takes as its focus the individual manager rather than the total enterprise. CSFs are elicited from a wide cross-section of managers in the organisation's main functional areas. When collected together these personal CSFs can then be refined into a set of organisational CSFs which 'allows a clear definition of the amount of management information which must be collected by the organisation.' 'The method centres on the information needs for management control where data is needed to monitor and to improve existing areas of business.' (Rockart (1979).

Rockart (1979) suggests that interviews with individual managers should be conducted over two to three sessions. In the first session the executive's goals are recorded and the CSFs which underlie those goals are discussed. Rockart (1979) suggests that there are four prime sources of CSFs:

- the structure of the industry,
- competitive strategy,
- temporal changes – those areas which are important at that particular time,
- environmental factors – such as changes in government and economy.

Clearly, the success factors will change over time but the manager is asked to focus on those areas which are vital to the period for which he/she is planning. The analyst then sharpens up the CSFs and the second session is used to review the results of the first session and measures to determine the success of these critical success factors. From these CSFs it is possible to determine the information (both internal and external) which is necessary to support the decisions which need to made by that particular manager in the critical areas and the analyst also discusses how to customise the reports and other information which the manager receives to meet his/her particular needs within the constraints imposed upon him/her. If necessary a third session is used to review the CSF measures and reporting sequence. The advantage of the method is that executives can see the usefulness of it, it feels appropriate, he/she is able to customise the information he/she receives so the data can be 'cut' in ways which are appropriate on each instance he/she uses the information. It takes into account that the fact that executives' information needs will vary from manager to manager and that for an individual they will vary over time. The process of analysing the CSFs in itself is valuable because it forces the manager to focus on those areas which are critical and to determine those measures which can measure the success. The method also limits the amount of information which needs to be collected and highlights the need for constant reassessment of information needs in the light of changes in the business environment.

CONCLUSION

The manager has a considerable need for information but he/she often has considerable difficulty in obtaining that information. There are several reasons for this, some of which are concerned with what appears to be the manager's difficulty in recognising and defining his/her information needs. Other reasons are concerned with what seems to be a misunderstanding by those charged with the provision and mediation of information to management of what information might be useful to managers. The result is often frustration and recriminations for both the manager and for those charged with catering for information needs, with a consequent detriment to the performance of the organisation as a whole.

BIBLIOGRAPHY

Abell, Angela and Winterman, Vivienne. 'Introduction and Background,' in *Information Culture and Business Performance*, edited by Anne Grimshaw (Hatfield: University of Hertfordshire Press, 1995).

Ackoff, Russell L. 'Management Misinformation Systems.' *Management Science* 14, 1967, pp. B147-B157.

Aguilar, Francis Joseph. *Scanning the Business Environment* (New York: Macmillan, 1967).

Crockett, Fess. 'Revitalizing Executive Information Systems.' *Sloan Management Review*, Summer 1992, pp. 39-47.

Daft, Richard L., Sormunen, Juhani, and Parks, Don. 'Chief Executive Scanning, Environmental Characteristics, and Company Performance: an empirical study.' *Strategic Management Journal* 9, 1988, pp. 123-139.

Davenport, T.H. and Prusak, L. 'Blow Up the Corporate Library.' *International Journal of Information Management* 13, 1993, pp. 405-412.

Davies, G.B. 'Strategies for Information Requirements Determination.' *IBM Systems Journal* 1, 1982, pp. 4-30.

Drucker, Peter. 'The Information Executives Truly Need.' *Harvard Business Review*, January/February 1995, pp. 54-62.

Feldman, Martha S. and March, James G. 'Information in Organisations as Signal and Symbol.' *Administrative Science Quarterly* 26, 1981, pp. 171-186.

Forrester, J. *Industrial Dynamics* (Boston: MIT Press, 1961)

Ghoshal, Sumantra and Kim, Seok Ki. 'Building Effective Intelligence Systems for Competitive Advantage.' *Sloan Management Review*, Fall 1986, pp. 49-58.

Ginman, Mariam. 'Information Culture and Business Performance.' *IATUL Quarterly* 2, 1988, pp. 93-106.

Gorry, G. Anthony and Scott Morton, Michael S. 'A Framework for Management Information Systems.' *Sloan Management Review,* Fall 1971, pp. 55-70.

Howard, Geoffrey S. and Weinroth, G. Jay. 'Users' Complaints: information system problems from the users' perspective.' *Journal of Systems Management,* May 1987, pp. 30-34.

Iselin, Errol. 'The Impact of Information Diversity on Information Overload: effects in unstructured managerial decision-making.' *Journal of Information Science* 15, 1989, pp. 163-173.

Isenberg, Daniel J. 'How Managers Think.' *Harvard Business Review,* November/December 1984, pp. 81-90.

Jacoby, Jacob, Speller, Donald E. and Kohn, Carol A. 'Brand Choice Behaviour as a Function of Information Load.' *Journal of Marketing Research,* February 1974, pp. 63-69.

Kanter, Jerry. 'Guidelines for Attaining Information Literacy.' *Information Strategy: The Executive's Journal,* Spring 1996, pp. 6-11.

KPMG Peat Marwick Management Consultants. *Information for Strategic Management: a survey of leading companies* (London: KPMG Peat Marwick Management Consultants, 1990).

Larson, Erik W. and King, Jonathan B. 'The Systematic Distortion of Information: an ongoing challenge to management.' *Organisational Dynamics,* 1992, pp. 49-61.

McGee, James V. and Prusak, Laurence. *Managing Information Strategically* (New York: John Wiley & Sons, 1992).

McKinnon, Sharon M. and Bruns, William J. *The Information Mosaic* (Boston: Harvard Business School Press, 1992).

Mintzberg, Henry. 'The Myth of MIS.' *California Management Review,* Fall 1972, pp. 92-97.

Mintzberg, Henry. *Impediments to Use of Management Information* (New York and Hamilton, Ontario: National Association of Accountants and The Society of Industrial Accountants of Canada, 1975).

Munro, Malcolm C. and Wheeler, Basil R. 'Planning Critical Success Factors in Management Information Requirements.' *MIS Quarterly,* December 1980, pp. 27-38.

Munro, Malcolm C. 'Determining the Manager's Information.' *Journal of Systems Management,* June 1978, pp. 34-39.

Newall, Allen and Simon, Herbert. *Human Problem Solving* (Englewood Cliffs, N.J.: Prentice Hall, 1972).

Owens, Ian and Wilson, T.D. 'Information and Business Performance: a study of information systems and services in high performing companies.' *Journal of Librarianship and Information Science* 29(1), 1997, pp. 19-28.

Porter M. and Miller, V. 'How Information Gives You a Competitive Advantage.' *Harvard Business Review,* July/August 1985, pp. 149-160.

Porter, M. *Competitive Strategy: techniques for analyzing industries and competitors* (New York: Free Press, 1980).

Porter, M. *Competitive Advantage: creating and sustaining superior performance* (New York: Free Press, 1985).

Radecki, C.M. and Jaccard, J. 'Perceptions of Knowledge, Actual Knowledge, and Information Search Behaviour.' *Journal of Experimental Social Psychology* 31, 1995, pp. 107-138.

Reuters Business Research. *To Know or Not to Know: the politics of information* (London: Reuters, 1994).

Reuters Business Research. *Dying for Information* (London: Reuters, 1996).

Rockart, John F. 'Chief Executives Define their own Data Needs.' *Harvard Business Review,* March /April 1979, pp. 81-93.

Rowe, A.J. *Managerial Decision-making (Modules in Management)* (Chicago: Science Research Associates, 1984).

Schneider, Susan C. 'Information Overload: causes and consequences.' *Human Systems Management* 7, 1987, pp. 143-153.

Simon, H. 'A Behavioural Model of Rational Choice.' *Quarterly Journal of Economics* 64(1), 1955.

Simon, H.A. *Models of Man* (New York: John Wiley and Sons, 1957).

Simon, H.A. *Administrative Behaviour* (Basingstoke: Macmillan, 1960).

Straw, Barry M., Sandelands, Lance E. and Dutton, Jane E. 'Threat-Rigidity Effects in Organisational Behaviour: a multilevel analysis.' *Administrative Science Quarterly* 26, 1981, pp. 501-524.

Taylor, Robert S. *Value-added Processes in Information Systems* (Norwood: Ablex Publishing, 1986).

Wildavsky, Aaron. 'Information as an Organisational Problem.' *Journal of Management Studies* 20, 1983, pp. 29-40.

Wilson, Tom and Walsh, Christina. *Information Behaviour: an interdisciplinary perspective* (London: British Library, British Library Research and Innovation Report 10, 1995).

Note

1   Later writers often refer to programmed decision as 'structured decisions' and to unprogrammed decisions as 'unstructured decisions'.

Chapter 4

Sources of managerial information

INTRODUCTION

In a dynamic business environment, managers have a continuing need for up-to-date, accurate, timely, relevant information but it would appear that in many organisations the formal systems such as library and information units and computerised information systems originally designed to cater for this need are clearly failing to do so. As was reported previously, much of the information required for operational control is provided largely as a by-product of the operational processes themselves or from other internal sources; similarly, much of the information for management and tactical control consists largely of summarised reports of internal processes. Strategic information, which is sourced largely from external rather than internal sources and should, therefore, be readily available from an organisation's library and information unit, seems equally difficult to provide. Managers, however, seem to obtain reliable information which enables them to remain, in Mintzberg's (1973) words, 'the nerve centre of the organisation's information'. This chapter investigates the actual sources which managers use to obtain information and considers the role of formal and informal, and personal and impersonal sources of information and the media which make it available.

THE EXTERNAL ENVIRONMENT AND THE COLLECTION OF INFORMATION

The importance of the external environment makes the collection of information about that environment essential. The external environment, perhaps more than any other factor, affects structure of the organisation, its internal processes, the decisions it makes and the way in which makes those decisions. Global competition, environmental factors such as volatility of exchange rates, changes in public policy, shorter product life cycles, deregulation and the convergence of technologies have increased the complexity of the business environment. As Ghosal and Kim (1986) point out, in many sectors competitive positions are now determined not on the basis of a technological breakthrough as in the past but on the basis of how well the organisation can cope with the current wave of change. An information advantage about business opportunities and problems may depend on management's recognition of signals that other organisations may miss. The collection of relevant information about this environment and the development of successful mechanisms to do this materially affect the performance of an organisation. This results in a large increase in the collection of information about the external environment and in the processing of that information within the organisation as managers seek to identify opportunities and problem areas and implement strategic or structural adaptations to take account of that environment.

ENVIRONMENTAL SCANNING

Organisations collect information from the external world and this process is called 'environmental scanning'. Aguilar (1967) defines environmental scanning as 'Scanning for information about events and relationships in a company's outside environment, the knowledge of which would assist top management in its task of charting the company's future course of action'.

In ordinary parlance 'to scan' means to look over something quickly, but environmental scanning can mean several things; it may range from gathering data in a deliberate fashion, such as of the kind which results from extensive market research, to a directed conversation over lunch or the chance observation of a colleague or other person.

The scanning process

There are several ways in which the organisation may scan the environment for information, some of which are more formal than others:

- Surveillance mode – Aguilar (1967) refers to this as a kind of undirected exposure to information with no specific decision or purpose in mind. The sources used for such surveillance are varied but one of the most popular is the newspaper. Many managers read a newspaper every day and, as the Reuters survey (1994) reported, many managers say that the newspaper is regarded as one of the most important sources of information. Much of the information gleaned from such sources is immediately forgotten and much of the rest is only distantly related to matters of current concern to the manager. For instance, it may be of general interest to a manager that there is a presidential election in America within three years but it is not of immediate concern unless they have business dealings which make it important. Nearer the date, however, the election may become more significant since it may produce uncertainty in the American markets in which the organisation does business.

  The sheer amount of available information, however, means that even in surveillance mode it is impossible for the manager to scan everything. Inevitably, there is some selection and filtering of sources and material by the manager and his/her choice of material is likely to reflect his/her general interests, experience and political and economic biases. As reported above, however, this may lead to a distorted view of the world and the result is that it is even less likely that the manager will be exposed to material which substantially contradicts his/her view of the world. This may be detrimental to the organisation.

- Conditioned viewing – this type of scanning is more directed and deliberate than surveillance. Aguilar (1967) says that in this mode of scanning the manager usually knows the type of information he/she is looking for as he/she may already have been alerted to it by some event. Thus, if a manager hears a rumour about a competitor, he/she is likely to be more sensitive to such information when he/she is exposed to material from other sources such as newspapers and the television.

- Informal search – this is a relatively limited and unstructured effort to obtain specific information according to Aguilar (1967). Colleagues and other information providing functions within the organisation may be advised that the manager is interested in the topic and requested to 'keep an eye out' for it. He/she may request that he/she receives press cuttings on the topic, he/she might even act in a manner likely to improve the chances of encountering the required information. For instance, he/she may attend meetings, lectures or conferences.

- Formal search – Aguilar (1967) says that in this mode of scanning there is a deliberate effort to secure the desired information. It may involve a request to an information unit to institute a formal search for specific information relating to the issue; this might include a search of internal and external databases, external information brokers, visits to external organisations such as trade and professional libraries. The request for information may be more specific and might involve a Companies House search or a patent search.

Formal searching and scanning

Many organisations collect information in a very ad hoc way – information is used if it happens to be relevant and comes to the attention of someone in a position to use it. Given the complexity of the current business environment this seems surprising; a complex environment would seem to call for systematic scanning of the environment. However, there is much potentially useful information about the environment available externally which the organisation might make use of. Formal scanning, however, may be very costly and so costs must be weighed against the perceived benefits. This causes a problem because the benefits of formal scanning are not immediately obvious and in many instances will be largely unquantifiable. (Nor, of course, is it possible to quantify the costs of inappropriate decisions or missed opportunities based on inadequate information if the organisation does not scan the external environment.) Obvious benefits from scanning will depend on the relevance of the information to the organisational task or goal related activity, issue or plan. It is likely, therefore, that the organisation will only institute formal scanning procedures where it foresees that the expense will be outweighed by the benefit. The criteria an organisation uses to determine which issues are likely to satisfy this condition will probably, according to Aguilar (1967), include the following:

- Urgency or timeliness of the issue – if the issue impinges very seriously on the ability of the organisation to produce, the issue is likely to be regarded as in need of urgent attention. For instance, the issue may affect supplies of raw materials which in turn will affect production and hence sales. In such circumstances the issue will be regarded as sufficiently important that the benefits of instituting formal scanning procedures are likely to outweigh the costs.

- Perception of the issue as a current or potential problem – the perception of an issue as a current or potential problem, such as political instability in a country from which raw materials are sourced, will raise the profile of the issue and the institution of formal scanning procedures is likely to be considered.

- Likely impact of the issue on the organisation's long-term plans – if the issue is perceived to have an impact on the long-term plans of the organisation this may affect its strategy and the issue may thus be perceived as requiring the urgent attention of the organisation – for instance, the merger of two erstwhile competitors or the entry into the market of a new organisation or a change in business conditions.

The factors listed above relate to the perceived importance of the issue and its impact, but according to Aguilar (1967), other factors will also determine whether formal scanning procedures are instituted:

- The extent to which the organisation can define the problem as an issue for which informational needs are definable. Not all problems can be solved by the collection and processing of information. For instance, for strategic problems it is not always obvious which questions the organisation should be asking, so the collection of information with which to solve them may not arise. Obviously, the easier it is to define precisely what information is required, the more likely it is that a formal search will be instituted and the more affordable it will be seen to be.

- The amount of appropriate information which the organisation has already collected on the topic – many organisations systematically collect information about potentially relevant matters such as customers, competitors and the business environment. An important issue involving a customer, for instance, may be resolved by consulting the available information rather then instituting a further formal search.

- The extent to which members of the organisation believe that information is available on a topic – there has been a massive increase in the information available about the external environment and few managers are aware of this and may not realise how quickly such information can be provided or how useful it might be. For instance, it is possible to locate information on companies in the Republic of China and some of the developing nations but few managers are aware of this and consequently may not request that a formal search be instituted to locate such information.

- The level of seniority and amount of influence wielded by the person suggesting the issue – the likelihood that a formal search will be regarded worthwhile may also depend on the seniority of the person who requests the search. The more senior and influential they are (or are perceived to be), the more likely that a formal search will be considered worthwhile.

Some factors may positively militate against the institution of a formal search:

- The amount of time available – if the information is required immediately then there may not be sufficient time in which to institute a formal search.

- Availability of resources – there may not be resources available to institute a formal search. The organisation might not be able to make the necessary manpower available and might not be prepared to spend the money which is required to brief an information broker on the information required. Indeed, the use of a broker may not even be considered because of the confidentiality of the issue.

- Necessary facilities required for formal scanning may not be available in the organisation – these may take the form of research tools such as databases, books, journals etc. and/or skilled staff to use these resources.

- Organisational politics may preclude a formal search – senior managers may refuse a formal search as it may throw up information which goes against some of their vested interests. For instance, information may be discovered which threatens their position or casts doubt on their competence.

Once the information has been collected by formal scanning processes, it seems reasonable to speculate that it is assessed in some way to determine its usefulness in the decision-making process. One may further speculate that the more adequate the data, the less impetus there will be to initiate further formal scanning, though it seems likely that conditioned viewing and probably informal searching will continue if only for the reason that this will keep the decision-maker up-to-date with events. One might also speculate that where information gathered as a result of a formal search proves less than adequate or perhaps contrary to what was expected then, depending on circumstances such as the personality of decision-maker and the confidence that he/she has in those doing the scanning, further searches will either be abandoned or other sources will be probed for the information.

Informal scanning

In circumstances where it is considered inappropriate to institute a formal scan, Aguilar (1967) reports that scanning is conducted using less formal methods such as directed viewing or informal searching and the issue will become one of the many issues that are noticed during surveillance of newspapers and other sources. Such information might be of the type, 'I need information on competitor product development' or on political developments in a major export market. Indeed, not only would formal methods cost too much for the collection of information such as this, such methods are unlikely to produce satisfactory results, regardless of the amount of money spent on its collection. Such questions do not lend themselves to formal scanning methods since the manager is looking to be alerted to the change in events rather than the current state of events.

In the course of undirected viewing an issue may be highlighted which is regarded as important – this may be a problem, an opportunity or, for instance, information on a competitor which is seen as relevant to organisational goals or tasks. At such a time the organisation may review the information it already has available on the issue. If the information available is sufficient then it is likely that no further action will be taken, though it is likely that the highlighting of the issue will ensure that its appearance in the newspapers at a later date will ensure that it is noticed by managers acting in surveillance mode. If the organisation agrees, however, Aguilar (1967) reports, that the issue is of sufficient importance that further information is required then a higher form of scanning may be triggered, the particular types determined by the criteria outlined above. In any event, it seems likely that the organisation will have become more sensitive to the issue and any additional information may lead to a further upgrading in the scanning mode.

Similarly, an issue which is perceived as less important may be dropped from the scanning system altogether. The length of time informational needs remain in the system varies greatly. However, an organisation is likely to have an ongoing need to monitor its competitors, markets, customers and suppliers at the very least, and such information needs are likely to lead to a systematisation of scanning activities. For instance, the organisation may subscribe to a press cuttings agency and request all cuttings from whatever sources on these issues. Other issues may initially seem important but cease to be so and care must be taken that requests for information are regularly checked to ensure that they are in line with organisational needs. New issues require information while old issues cease to be relevant; it is, for instance, very easy to continue to receive information about a client or customer long after such business has been lost.

Provided the right information is obtained, scanning behaviour remains unchanged but if the system fails to provide for the needs and desires for information, and especially if the organisation has fallen into difficulties, then changes can be expected in scanning behaviour. Aguilar (1967) reports that such changes may involve a change in the mode of scanning; thus undirected viewing may be upgraded to formal search and/or a change may be made in the procedures which are followed for each mode – thus a formal search may be redefined to use an external information broker as well as internal resources.

What information is obtained by organisations during the scanning process?

The organisation needs to achieve a compromise between the desires of the organisation and the constraints imposed by the external environment and so it requires information which will enable it to resolve that compromise in ways which are as advantageous as possible to itself. For many managers systematic environmental scanning involves dividing the external environment into sectors, attempting to determine the key variables or critical success factors for their particular organisation in each of the sectors and then attempting to collect that information in either a systematic or ad hoc fashion. Ideally, the retrieved information is interpreted for a variety of purposes including decision-making and problem-solving and ultimately the information may be integrated into the strategic plan.

There is considerable agreement among writers about the categorisation of information requirements in organisations. Aguilar (1967) and Auster and Choo (1993), for instance, choose the following categories:

- Customer information – this category includes information about those organisations or individuals which purchase the products or services of the company. It includes final customers as well as those who purchase for resale. The information collected might include details of demand for the products and services, exports, information on the current and potential market capacity, information on customers and potential customers, their preferences and their problems.

- Competition information – this category will include information about competing products, financial and market information on competing firms, their tactics and capabilities. It should also include information on companies which make products or services which while not of the same kind as the organisation might be substituted for their products and services. For instance, gas can be substituted for coal in some markets, so gas companies must be regarded as competitors for firms in the coal industry.

- Industry and sectoral information – this category includes information about industrial and sectoral policy; structural changes such as mergers, acquisitions and joint ventures; new entrants; leads for mergers and joint ventures.

- Technology and processes – the business environment is so dynamic that an organisation which wishes to compete successfully must use the most cost-effective and efficient methods of production. Organisations require information about developments in production techniques and methods; innovative use of raw materials; new materials and trends in research and development. They will also need to know about new patents and licensing agreements.

- General economic considerations – the general economic climate affects the ability of an organisation to compete, so organisations may require information about exchange rates which may affect their ability to export and import, and changes in fiscal policy may affect their financial position, as well as a wide variety of other economic information. The increased globalisation of business results in a need to be aware of the outlook for business not only in their own nation but also internationally.

- Specific economic climate – information about the specific economic climate in which an organisation does business is also of interest; of particular importance are the costs of raw materials and prices for current and potential products for its own and competing companies. Information about the availability and costs of resources such as labour and land is also essential.

- Regulatory factors – all sectors of business are subject to regulation by government legislation. Such regulation may be in the form of health and safety rules, employment legislation and planning regulations. In addition, specific industries may be required to comply with rules and regulations imposed either by governments or by trade and professional associations. For instance, the financial services sector is governed by legislation concerning the selling of financial products, and the fishing industry is regulated by quotas imposed by European law. Failure to comply with such rules and regulations may result in the imposition of severe sanctions and most organisations have systems in place which ensure the collection and processing of information about rules and regulations which affect them.

- Sociocultural factors – factors such as changes in the demographic make-up of an area may cause considerable disruption for organisations. Fewer school leavers may result in fewer young people available to take up apprenticeships; changes in the social values of the workforce may affect their willingness to work overtime. The increase in the number of women in the workforce may require the organisation to rethink some of its procedures and facilities, for instance the provision of a subsidised crèche may be very attractive if there is a shortage of labour. Information about sociocultural factors may be regarded as essential for the planning of the future of the organisation.

While most organisations seek some kinds of information, some of the information is regarded as more important than the rest. Aguilar (1967) reports that, regardless of size and industry sector, most organisations regard what he refers to as 'market tidings' as particularly important – this is information on customers, competitors and the sector in which the organisation does business. This is not surprising; this type of information provides a kind of common denominator for managers throughout the organisation, regardless of their functional responsibilities or place in the organisational hierarchy. The success or failure of the organisation, and hence, ultimately, their jobs, depends on the ability of the organisation to compete. Market tidings inform the members of the organisation about the success of their efforts and those of their competitors, so such information is the focal point of their common interest; it is information to which they can all relate and recognise as significant.

Initiating scanning activity

As the complexity and the rate of change in the organisation's business sector increases, the amount of uncertainty perceived by top managers also increases. Writers such as Daft, Sormunen and Parks (1988) and Auster and Choo (1993) have shown that there is evidence that, as the members of the organisation perceive that the uncertainty in their business environment is increasing, they increase the amount of environmental scanning. However, uncertainty by itself will not lead to scanning behaviour. Unless the external events are perceived as important to organisational performance, managers will have little interest in them. In areas of the organisation regarded as of high importance, external events are perceived to be directly linked to operations and performance. Uncertainty and perceived importance together create what is defined as strategic uncertainty, and it is likely that this combination creates an increased need for policy makers to scan events in selected environmental sectors.

Environmental scanning is (or should be) intimately tied up with the decision-making processes within the organisation. Necessarily it is an incomplete and imperfect process because the outside world is a complex and dynamic place and it is often not obvious what information the organisation should seek. Indeed the more the organisation tries to cope with the dynamic environment by seeking more information and the further it moves from its own environment, the larger the number of variables with which it must cope. Information on current national competitors may be relatively easy to obtain but information on potential global competitors may be less easy to find and the possibility of loss of market share to such competitors may be compounded by variables other than price and service, such as exchange rates, cheap cost of local labour, subsidised transport and local rules and regulations.

Boundary spanning roles and scanning activity

In addition to the creation of units such as information units or Strategic Business Units, some organisations which recognise their need for information about the external world often charge specific individuals with the task of scanning the external environment. However, many other people may perform in the role of scanning the environment as part of their overall work for the organisation. For instance, managers collect information when they are visiting clients, customers and peers and disseminate it to relevant members of their own organisation. Such formal and informal roles are often referred to as boundary spanning roles because they span the boundary between the organisation and the environment. According to Aldrich and Herker (1977), people operating in these roles not only collect the information by scanning the environment but they also process it, filtering out what they believe to be superfluous or irrelevant to the organisation's needs and to those of its individual members. Such boundary scanners may put a different 'spin' on the information or simply pass on the information which they have acquired to relevant people within the organisation in an informal manner, perhaps by mentioning the issue to colleagues over lunch or by distributing it using a personal emailing list. Alternatively, the issue may be such that it warrants general dissemination through-out the organisation. In such a situation the boundary scanner may pass the information to those who can ensure the distribution of the information through the formal channels of the organisation such as the monthly newsletter or report or by placing details on the organisa-tion's intranet.

Clearly the role of boundary scanner, whether officially constituted or merely adopted, is a very important one. The organisation may rely on the information which this person collects and may base important decisions or solve problems based on the information is provided. The person who acts in this role, therefore, must necessarily be fairly sen-ior – part of the boundary spanning role is to filter out irrelevant information, which implies that the person performing this role requires an in-depth knowledge about the organisation and its aims and objec-tives. Such a person must also be senior enough to ensure that he/she is privy to those circles in which such information is provided, and he/she must have sufficient contacts in the external world to be able to collect relevant information.

In many organisations the members of the board and to a lesser extent other professionals (though this will depend on the industry) perform the boundary scanning roles. Some people make good scanners, oth-ers do not. Aguilar (1967) reports that to perform successfully in such a role requires intelligence, experience, ability, interest and a sensitivity to events and to the organisation for which he/she works. Often the best person to perform this role by virtue of his/her patience, knowl-edge, experience and availability may not be well-known to members of the board or perhaps not of proven competence in their eyes. In such circumstances the decision-makers may have difficulty in plac-ing their full confidence in such a person and in the information he/she obtains – especially if it runs counter to what they expect. In such cases, therefore, it is important that, somewhere in the information flow, the information provided by such a person is validated by at least one senior person in the organisation.

Situations in which managers might require information about the external world

Managers require information on the external world for a wide variety of tasks. Primarily, this section focuses on the collection of information for strategic planning and also information which triggers a business opportunity or galvanises the organisation into action. Mintzberg (1975) as we have seen, refers to the manager as 'an active information manipulator who works in a stimulus-response environment and fa-vours live action'. The stimulus may be a potential new customer or a new tactic by a competitor – anything which offers a business opportunity. To this end the manager seeks out hearsay, rumour and gossip because, as Mintzberg (1975) notes, 'today's gossip is tomorrow's fact'. Such 'trigger' information rarely finds its way into formal information systems and on those rare occasions on which it is made available, by the time it gets into the public domain the business opportunity which it offered will probably have been lost.

Sources of managerial information on the external environment

Several studies, such as those by McKinnon and Bruns (1992) and Taylor (1986), have been undertaken on the sources of managerial information and they classify the sources into those which are internal or external to the organisation and whether those sources are personal or impersonal. Personal sources are those sources which provide information directly to the manager, while impersonal sources are those sources which communicate information to a wide audience or through formal group activity.

Internal	External
Personal	*Personal*
subordinates	customers
peers	suppliers
superiors	business associates
other internal[2]	peers
	professional advisors[3]
Impersonal	*Impersonal*
reports	newspapers
memos	periodicals
scheduled company meetings	government publications
databases	trade and professional publications
intranet	web sites
	commercial databases
	annual reports
	clippings service
	television and radio
	advice agencies[4]

Figure 2 – Sources of information on the external environment[1]

KPMG (1990) surveyed managers about their use of external impersonal (formal) sources when formulating strategy. Their results were
surprising – 57% used industry journals, by far the highest number;
53% relied on newspapers and magazines; 49% used company annual
reports and 45% used analyst and banking reports. 43% of companies
did not use formal sources of external information when formulating
their strategy and KPMG (1990) report that in doing so they are operating in a vacuum and will, as a result, tend to react to events only when
they are almost forced to do so, instead of planning to allow for likely
contingencies and opportunities. Reuters (1994) and Auster and Choo
(1993), who looked at the sources of information which managers use
for purposes other than strategy also report a strong preference for
newspapers. Auster and Choo (1993) point out that a newspaper offers
the opportunity not only to address specific problems but also to get a
wide view of the business environment and check for information
which might trigger a business opportunity. Several writers, however,
have reported on the strong preference which managers exhibit for
personal rather than impersonal sources of information. Mintzberg
(1975) reports that managers prefer current information and move away
from formal reports and quantitative documents. Mintzberg (1972, 1973)
reports that managers systematically turn away from written reports
in favour of personal information sources and face-to-face discussions
Many other investigations report similar findings: Abell (1994) reports
that 'the primary information sources [for managers] were customers,
suppliers and business contacts', while Mckinnon and Bruns (1992)
report that 'personal discourse remains the primary channel for exchange of information in most companies'.

Preference for verbal media

From whom do managers obtain their verbal information?
As we have seen in chapter 2, one of the main roles of a manager is that
of information handler – indeed, Mintzberg (1972, 1973) refers to managers as information processing systems. In their roles as monitors,
disseminators and liaison personnel, they assume a primary role in
the information collection and processing in the organisation. The manager shows a marked preference for personal contact, however;
McKinnon and Bruns (1992) commented that 'all managers are con-
tinually seeking and giving information to others in ways that are
framed as social discourse'. This applies to both internal and external
personal contacts. The manager has much opportunity to gather information from internal personal contacts since, as Mintzberg (1972, 1973)
points out, he/she spends as much as a third to a half of their time
with subordinates and 10% of his time with superiors. He/she engages
in regular meetings with subordinates and superiors in his/her day-
to-day job. There is also great opportunity to gather intelligence from
external contacts since most managers spend as much as a third of their
time with external contacts. In his/her role as liaison person for his
organisation the manager builds up a network of external contacts by sit-
ting on committees, meeting peers, customers, suppliers and others.

Mintzberg (1972, 1973) goes on to say that the more dynamic the environment, the more the manager engages in informal communication. There is clearly much opportunity to collect information through gossip, hearsay and rumour and the manager develops a powerful personal database of external and internal information, much of which is current and non-documented. The information exchanged is both quantitative and qualitative and builds into a unique personal resource.

Why the preference for verbal information?
Abell (1994) suggests that managers prefer verbally mediated information because it is pre-digested. It is much easier and usually quicker to have someone explain something to you rather than having to read about it. McKinnon and Bruns (1992) suggest that the reason for the preference is that 'information from personal sources can be acted upon with confidence by the recipient because of the special relationship he or she has with the sender'.

Daft and Lengel (1984) suggest that there are other reasons why managers show a marked preference for face-to-face communication – the communication medium itself is information rich. Not only do media such as face-to-face communication offer the opportunity to exchange views but they provide the opportunity for instant feedback; misconceptions can be corrected, questions can be asked, points clarified and further information gained from the person's body language, voice and word choice. A face-to-face meeting will be imbued with rich emotions and the variety of language choice can be used to convey an understanding of a broader set of concepts and emotions. Face-to-face communication is the richest information medium but the telephone, though less rich, offers opportunities for feedback and correcting of misconceptions even though the visual cues are not available. Highly information rich media enable managers to make sense of complex topics in very short time scales. Many management problems are difficult and complex; hence formal sources of information are not rich enough to convey adequate insight and understanding; personal sources are much more insightful.

Written communication of the sort provided by reports and statistics are much less rich, feedback is slow, and visual cues are limited to the paper. The purpose of these written communications, which often take the form of reports, is usually to gather data on a subject, to synthesise and interpret it. Computer printouts of the sort provided by transaction processing systems (TPS) or management information systems (MIS) and similar systems are even less rich. The purpose of such documents is to provide data to enable managers to check that their department, or indeed the whole organisation, is likely to achieve its goals. They are largely control documents and pertain largely to the measurable aspects of the organisations.

Email and videoconferencing were not investigated by Daft and Lengel (1984) but one may speculate that email is less information rich than the telephone though more so than standard formal documents; while videoconferencing will be more rich than the phone since it permits visual cues but less rich than the face-to-face discussion since not all of the person is visible and their natural communication style is likely to be circumscribed to some extent by the intervention of the technology.

Daft, Lengel and Trevino (1987) say that managers should select the media which matches the message – when understanding is difficult good managers choose oral communications but when understanding is easier they prefer written media. Daft and Lengel (1984) suggest that the reasons managers often ignore formal sources and systematic studies is not personal ignorance, lack of training or personality defects, but rather that informal personal media are capable of providing richer information to managers about certain problems. Their conclusion is born out by Abell (1994), who reported that even when managers were offered the information they requested at no charge they still preferred to talk to someone face-to-face; she writes, 'although the firms confirmed that the information provided had been useful no firm was immediately converted to the use of such sources. Probably more useful were the introductions to other sources of information, to expertise or to the analysis of the information required'.

Information richness continuum
In the light of the above findings, Daft and Lengel (1984) propose what they refer to as the 'information richness continuum,' which they use to explain why different media are appropriate for different tasks.

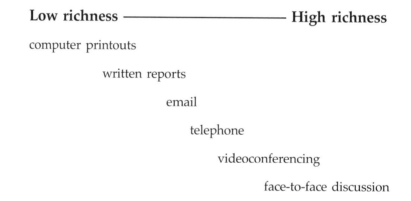

Figure 3 – Information richness continuum[5]

Information for managerial tasks

As we have seen, much of the information required for operational and managerial control tasks can be provided from internal sources and as such, organisations exert much control over how such information is structured, how it is mediated, who receives it, and what information the system provides. At the operational level there is a need for unambiguous information to answer questions such as 'How much coal are we using?', and 'How many items have we produced?' Uncertain situations usually result in an increase in the demand for and use of this largely quantitative information which is usually sufficient to satisfy requirements and provide the relevant answer since the answers required are usually a matter of fact rather than opinion. As McKinnon and Bruns (1992) report, such information is usually provided as a by-product of the transaction processing system itself. Similarly, the information which the manager uses to control the business is obtained from largely internal sources and is usually a matter of fact rather than opinion. Strategic information, on the other hand, is (or should be) obtained from sources which are largely external to the organisation and much of such information is subjective, based on opinion and speculation rather than fact. Trigger information (that which 'triggers' activity), according to Mintzberg (1975), is often also similarly based on opinion and speculation rather than solidly based in fact.

As we have seen, most managers spend some time on operational, control and strategic tasks and therefore are familiar with using the accurate quantitative information required for operational and control tasks as well as the speculative and less factually-based information which is required for strategic tasks and which may trigger entrepreneurial activity. Daft and Lengel (1984) suggest that different media are appropriate for the communication of information required for different tasks; they report that organisations use a variety of media, from those that are high in richness in situations in which they interface with the environment (environmental scanning and strategic planning) to media low in richness within the technical core (production, sales and other operational tasks). In general, organisations prefer to use media lower in richness for their day-to-day internal operations where there is little or no equivocality – it is as inappropriate to use a face-to-face discussion to pass on detailed quantitative data as it is to use a printout from a TPS for strategic planning. Daft and Lengel (1986) suggest that 'Organisations reduce equivocality through the use of sequentially less rich media down through the hierarchy.' It may be possible, therefore, to make some suggestions about the types of information required for the different categories of management activity:

- Operational tasks and management control tasks – information required for such tasks is usually simple; it is rarely necessary for those in receipt of such information to need to ask any supplementary questions. Such information, therefore, lends itself well to written media. There are usually procedural rules, regulations and policies to be followed which are carefully laid down in manuals or policies for each eventuality likely to be encountered at the operational and control level and so little initiative is required, merely simply rule-following by employees. Information for such tasks is relatively easy to communicate; it often takes the form of printouts from transaction processing systems and management information systems or the information may be communicated in reports, memos or email.

- Strategic and trigger tasks – Daft and Lengel (1984) use the word 'equivocal' to describe the dynamic and ambiguous nature of the business environment of the manager charged with the task of charting the future of the business and locating business opportunities. 'Equivocal' means that there is a lack of understanding and confusion about the environment; it is not clear which questions to ask, let alone what the solutions may be. It is a situation in which a search for further information is as likely to add to the confusion as to clarify it. In such a situation different people will have differing perspectives on the problem and it is these differing perspectives and the opportunity for discussion and feedback which are of interest to the manager. New data may be exchanged, but the advantage of meetings is to reach a collective judgment based on many differing perspectives and hence build understanding and cohesion within the group. When such initial difficulties are sorted out then less rich media may be used to communicate information.

CONCLUSION

The marked preference for verbal media which managers demonstrate in much of their information collecting activity would seem to be caused by the uncertain nature of their business environment and their need to obtain feedback from others which may confirm or deny their own perceptions of the situation. Similarly, in their search for business opportunities, managers seem to recognise that, with the exception of the newspaper, many formal sources are unlikely to prove fruitful. This finding about the information-seeking habits of managers may help to explain why so few managers perceive that the sources provided by formally constituted facilities such as libraries and information units are useful.

BIBLIOGRAPHY

Abell, Angela. 'Information Use and Business Success: a review of recent research of effective information delivery,' in *The Value and Impact of Information,* edited by Mary Feeney and Maureen Grieves (East Grinstead: Bowker-Saur, 1994).

Aguilar, Francis Joseph. *Scanning the Business Environment* (New York: Macmillan, 1967).

Aldrich, Howard and Herker, Diane. 'Boundary Spanning Roles and Organisational Structure.' *Academy of Management Review,* April 1977, pp. 217-230.

Auster, Ethel and Choo, Chun. 'Environmental Scanning by Chief Executive Officers in Two Canadian Industries.' *Journal of the American Society for Information Science* 44(4), 1993, pp. 194-203.

Choo, Chun Wei. 'Perception and Use of Information Sources by Chief Executives in Environmental Scanning.' *LISR* 16, 1994, pp. 23-40.

Daft, Richard L. and Lengel, Robert H. 'Information Richness: a new approach to managerial behaviour and organisational design.' *Research in Organisational Behaviour* 6, 1984, pp. 191-233.

Daft, Richard L. and Lengel, Robert H. 'Organisational Information Requirements, Media Richness and Structural Design.' *Management
Science* 32, 1986, pp. 554-571.

Daft, Richard L. Lengel, Robert H. and Trevino, Linda Klebe. 'Message
Equivocality, Media Selection, and Manager Performance: implications for information systems.' *MIS Quarterly,* September 1987,
pp. 355-366.

Daft, Richard L., Sormunen, Juhani, and Parks, Don. 'Chief Executive
Scanning, Environmental Characteristics, and Company Performance: an empirical study.' *Strategic Management Journal* 9, 1988, pp.
123-139.

Drucker, Peter. 'The Information Executives Truly Need.' *Harvard Business Review,* January/February 1995, pp. 54-62.

Feldman, Martha S. and March, James G. 'Information in Organisations
as Signal and Symbol.' *Administrative Science Quarterly* 26, 1981, pp.
171-186.

Ghoshal, Sumantra and Kim, Seok Ki. 'Building Effective Intelligence
Systems for Competitive Advantage.' *Sloan Management Review,* Fall
1986, pp. 49-58.

Gorry, G. Anthony and Scott Morton, Michael S. 'A Framework for Management Information Systems.' *Sloan Management Review,* Fall 1971,
pp. 55-70.

Keegan, Warren J. 'Multi-national Scanning: a study of the information
sources utilised by headquarters executives in multinational companies.' *Administrative Science Quarterly,* 1974, pp. 411-421.

KPMG Peat Marwick Management Consultants. *Information for Strategic Management: a survey of leading companies* (London: KPMG Peat
Marwick Management Consultants, 1990).

McGee, James V. and Prusak, Laurence. *Managing Information Strategically* (New York: John Wiley & Sons, 1992).

McKinnon, Sharon M. and Bruns, William J. *The Information Mosaic* (Boston: Harvard Business School Press, 1992).

Mintzberg, Henry. 'The Myth of MIS.' *California Management Review,* Fall
1972, pp. 92-97.

Mintzberg, Henry. *The Nature of Managerial Work* (New York: Harper
and Row, 1973).

Mintzberg, Henry. 'The Manager's Job, Folklore or Fiction.' *Harvard
Business Review,* July/August 1975, pp. 49-61.

Preble, J.F., Rau, P.A. and Reichel, A. 'The Environmental Scanning Practices of U.S. Multinationals in the late 1980s.' *MIR* 28, 1988, pp. 4-14.

Reuters Business Research. *To Know or Not to Know: the politics of information* (London: Reuters, 1994).

Reuters Business Research. *Dying for Information* (London: Reuters,
1996).

Taylor, Robert S. *Value-added Processes in Information Systems* (Norwood:
Ablex Publishing Corporation, 1986).

Notes

1   The list should not be regarded as exhaustive.

2   For instance, the sales force.

3   Bankers, lawyers, management consultants, accountants etc.

4   For instance, Business Link, DTI.

5   Based on Daft & Lengel but with email and videoconferencing added to the original model.

Chapter 5

Characteristics of useful information

INTRODUCTION

For many people the notion that good information should lead to improved decision-making seems intuitively obvious, and, indeed, there is research to support this (Porat & Haas (1969), Streufert (1973)). However, there are difficulties in determining what constitutes 'good' information. Several writers (for instance, Taylor (1986), Choo (1994), Mintzberg (1975), Crockett (1992), Zmud (1978)) have commented on the characteristics of 'good' information and many readers will be familiar with them; they include relevance, timeliness, appropriateness and comprehensiveness. These attributes are almost a mantra among information professionals and they have also found their way into the management and computer science professional press. In the light of what has been reported above about how managers seek information, however, and indeed, what researchers know about managers' preferred sources of information, it is appropriate that some re-examination of the value of these attributes should be undertaken as there appears to be some discrepancy between what those charged with the provision of information believe are desirable characteristics of information and what managers appear to require of their information. For instance, in the best of all possible worlds, comprehensiveness might be regarded as a desirable attribute of information, but so many managers indicate that they are already suffering from information overload that one is tempted to think that if comprehensive information means more information provision then they are unlikely to agree that the provision of comprehensive information on a subject is desirable.

While it is likely, therefore, that information required for operational tasks and management control tasks should possess the attribute of comprehensiveness, few managers are likely to regard it as a useful attribute of strategic or trigger information.

THE ATTRIBUTES OF INFORMATION LIKELY TO BE USEFUL TO MANAGERS

So what constitutes 'good' information? What are the attributes of information which make the information useful to managers?

- Relevant information – few would disagree that to be perceived as useful a piece of information must be relevant. It is not possible to define what constitutes 'relevant' information in any other than the most general terms, however, since even when two people are working on the same task they may not perceive the same information to be relevant. Relevant information is that information which is needed with respect to the current task(s) or is perceived as likely to be useful in the future because it can be used to further the aims and goals of the organisation or help the recipient make sense of the complex business environment. Relevancy also subsumes several other attributes:

- Timeliness – timely information is information which arrives at the appropriate time. It should not arrive before it is required nor when it is too late to act upon it.

- Accuracy – it seems obvious that one of the main characteristics of information is that it should be accurate. Useful information will pertain as closely as possible to the truth because few managers have the time to check all the information they need to use. Clearly for operational and management control purposes information must be accurate. The information collected for these tasks is largely quantitative and is often collected as a by-product of the operational process itself. It is possible to obtain very accurate information about these operational tasks and processes and this is essential because such information is often used to monitor performance and to determine whether the organisation is progressing towards its aims and objectives. It is also used as a basis for discussion on how such achievement might be improved. Clearly, managers will seek high accuracy in information which is to be used for such a purpose; indeed, the Hawley Committee (1995) recommends audit trails to verify the accuracy of such information. However, accuracy may not be such an important attribute of strategic or trigger information. Indeed, as we have seen, much of the information which comes into the organisation is ambiguous and complex and it may often be impossible to obtain completely accurate information. The manager thrives on gossip and hearsay in the relentless pursuit of the business opportunity and such information may be very difficult to authenticate but this does not necessarily devalue its usefulness for the manager. So, while accurate information must be seen as desirable, the search for completely accurate strategic or trigger information is unlikely to be cost-effective and it may be that to strive for such accuracy will delay action and may result in missed opportunities.

- Reliability of the information source – the attribute of reliability of the information source is more than a restatement of the attribute of accuracy of the information. A reliable information source is an information source which is perceived by the manager as authoritative and dependable: it is a source which the manager personally trusts and may possibly be a person with whom he/she has a personal relationship. Consequently, it seems that the information received from such a source is also perceived as reliable (and the implication is, therefore, that the information is accurate). Where the information source is a personal one – such as a colleague or a peer – then the credibility, status and reputation of the person providing the information will be an important determinant of whether or not the information they provide will be acted upon. It is possible, therefore, that a manager will act on information which is incorrect because he/she has received it from a source which he/she believed to be reliable.

- Good quality information – much is made of the importance of 'quality' as an attribute of information. The notion of quality includes many of the attributes listed above – accuracy, relevancy, timeliness. KPMG (1990) found that managers were on the whole satisfied with the quality of the information they received from organisational systems which was used to monitor performance (i.e. for management control tasks – internal information) but a significant majority were dissatisfied with important aspects of the quality of the information which they received to provide for their strategic needs.

- Good quality information sources – while managers state that they require good quality information, the use of good quality information sources appears not be quite such a high priority. Several writers have shown that most decision-makers have a preference for accessible sources of information rather than quality sources. Indeed, Oreilley (1982) reports the perhaps more startling results that even though most managers were able to identify the high quality sources of information in respect to a particular issue, in practice they tended to use sources of a lesser quality more frequently. Similar results have been shown among other disciplines – Menzel and Katz (1955) found that physicians tended to rely on the accessible drug salesmen rather than quality sources such as learned journals for their information on drug innovation. Yet the provision of quality information would seem to be the prime determinant of whether a source is regarded as a quality source; so it appears that even when they are provided with quality information sources, managers will only make use of such information from such sources if it is readily accessible. So, to believe that decisions are made in the light all available information is to ignore the totality of the manager's environment.

Oreilley (1982) suggests that there are several reasons for what seems to be a less than optimal choice of information source which may result in the likely outcome of less than optimal information, which may in turn lead to less than optimal decision-making:

- Decision-makers under time pressure incur costs in seeking out less accessible sources. To use the 'quality' source might involve a larger commitment of time than the manager feels able to give. To give that time might mean that the amount of time available to analyse the information is reduced, which in itself might impair the decision; alternatively, to give that commitment of time may result in some other pressing task not being performed which in itself might impair the effectiveness of the organisation as a whole.

- Access to quality information sources may be restricted because of costs, or because those sources are only available in a library for instance.

Oreilley (1982) suggests that as a consequence of this reduced accessibility, decision-makers come to rely on certain tried and tested sources of information which they perceive to be credible and trustworthy rather than sources which might objectively be regarded as quality sources. Taylor (1975) makes a similar point when he refers to the people's 'habitual pref-

erences for particular sources of information'. Yet many writers (for instance, Porat and Haas (1969) and Streufert (1973)) have reported that the
quality of the decision-making and managerial performance is affected
by the quality of the information used and clearly many managers are not
making use of the best quality information.

- Accessibility – as shown above, many managers regard the accessibility of information as more important than its quality.
  Accessibility is not just physical access to information, it includes
  factors such as:
  - knowing what is available,
  - knowing how to use what is available – for instance knowing
    how to use search agents, abstracts, indexes,
  - knowing who knows what.

However, while accessibility might be preferred to quality, clearly both
quality and accessibility will be the desired aim and this may help to
further explain the popularity of verbal sources of information. As we
have seen in chapter 4, a manager regards personal sources of information as largely reliable. (A reliable information source is one which
is perceived to be authoritative and dependable: it is a source which
the manager personally trusts.) As a consequence, the information from
such a source is likely to be perceived as reliable. Such 'reliable' information might also be seen as 'quality' information, particularly if the
personal source has access to otherwise restricted information and is
perceived to be an authoritative source and/or has status and a high
reputation. However, many personal sources will also be readily accessible – the manager is likely to have access to subordinates for most
of the working day and as he/she spends as much as a third of his
time with external contacts – clients, suppliers, peers – he/she also
has access to a considerable network of contacts, many of whom he/
she sees face-to-face regularly and most of whom are accessible on the
phone. Such personal sources are very information rich – the speak-
er's intonation provides information in addition to the words that are
spoken, the manager can obtain feedback, may ask questions and seek
further information. Such features make verbal sources not only accessible sources but they will also be perceived to be quality sources and
it seems likely that greater access to technologies such as email and
videoconferencing will make many such sources even more accessible and hence relied on even more than at present.

- Comprehensiveness of the information – sometimes referred to
  as completeness. The importance of complete and comprehensive information was highlighted in the Hawley Committee
  Report (1995). Clearly this is an essential attribute of information
  for operational/control information but one must question the
  usefulness of the pursuit of this attribute for information required
  for strategic tasks for several reasons:
  - A request for comprehensiveness in information suggests that
    there is some kind of ultimate truth which can be found if all
    the information is collected – for most subjects where some-

thing more than a simple request for data is required this is unlikely to be the case. Different sources will provide a different 'spin' on a topic; even knowledgeable commentators such as economists rarely agree about events. Much information about the external environment is likely to be complex, ambiguous and equivocal, so the search for comprehensive information is more likely to confuse than clarify.

- The costs to the manager in terms of both time and money of seeking further marginal information (however that may be defined) are likely to be prohibitive.

- The amount of information likely to be collected as a result of a search for comprehensive information is likely to render useful analysis impossible.

- The amount of information likely to be collected as a result of a search for comprehensive information will, in many instances, severely overload a manager and might result in personal stress. This is clearly demonstrated by Jacoby (1984), who showed that people have an optimal threshold for information and even a marginal increase in information provision, far from improving decisions, will actually lead to dysfunctional decision-making.

- Comprehensive gossip and hearsay is impossible. As we have seen, gossip and hearsay form an important part of a manager's information diet. Such information is particularly important to trigger action. However, while the manager might check a few details of any gossip he/she wishes to act upon, to fail to initiate action until comprehensive information was available on the topic would waste time and would almost certainly result in many lost opportunities.

- Predictiveness of the information – little regarded in the literature, it would be helpful if information used in strategic planning could inform about the future. Such information might include an indication of the probability of the occurrence of events, for instance. As Simpson and Prusak (1995) report, little information has this attribute.

- Presentation and format of the information – some formats are more appropriate than others for the presentation of particular information. Both Zmud (1978) and Crockett (1992) have indicated the importance of presentation in an understandable form when providing information to executives. Crockett (1992) goes on to suggest that with screen-based information, the ability to customise the way in which the information is viewed on screen using different formats, graphs and modeling systems will increase the usefulness of the information to the manager and this might improve the predictive value of the information.

CONCLUSION

It is very difficult to make definitive statements about the nature of information likely to be useful to managers in any other than very general terms. What one can say is that there are several attributes of a particular piece of information or an information source which help to determine whether the information is perceived as useful to a particular recipient. While it is possible to delineate the attributes which people require of their information or their information sources, the precise importance of each attribute is not only specific to each individual but is also likely to vary depending on the task in hand, the manager's personal style, and the amount of information the manager already has about the task or subject, so even for one individual the balance of desired information attributes required for different task will vary.

BIBLIOGRAPHY

Abell, Angela. 'Information Use and Business Success: a review of recent research of effective information delivery,' in *The Value and Impact of Information*, edited by Mary Feeney and Maureen Grieves (East Grinstead: Bowker-Saur, 1994).

Choo, Chun Wei. 'Perception and Use of Information Sources by Chief Executives in Environmental Scanning.' *LISR* 16, 1994, pp. 23-40.

Crockett, Fess. 'Revitalizing Executive Information Systems.' *Sloan Management Review,* Summer 1992, pp. 39-47.

Gerstenberger, P., and Allen, T. 'Criteria Used by Research and Development Engineers in the Selection of an Information Source.' *Journal of Applied Psychology* 52, 1969, pp. 272-279.

Hawley Committee. *Information as an Asset: a consultative report* (London: KPMG IMPACT Programme, 1995).

Jacoby, Jacob. 'Perspectives on Information Overload.' *Journal of Marketing Research* 10, 1984, pp. 432-435.

KPMG Peat Marwick Management Consultants. *Information for Strategic Management: a survey of leading companies* (London: KPMG Peat Marwick Management Consultants, 1990).

McGee, James V. and Prusak, Laurence. *Managing Information Strategically* (New York: John Wiley & Sons, 1992)

McKinnon, Sharon M. and Bruns, William J. *The Information Mosaic* (Boston: Harvard Business School Press, 1992).

Menzel, H. and Katz, E. 'Social Relations and Innovation in the Medical Profession.' *Public Opinion Quarterly* 19, 1955, pp. 337-353.

Mintzberg, Henry. *Impediments to Use of Management Information* (New York and Hamilton, Ontario: National Association of Accountants and The Society of Industrial Accountants of Canada, 1975).

Oreilley, Charles A. 'Variations in Decision Makers' Use of Information Sources: the impact of quality and accessibility of information.' *Academy of Management Journal* 25(4), 1982, pp. 756-771.

Porat , A. and Haas, J. 'Information Effects on Decision-making.' *Behavioural Science* 14, 1969, pp. 98-104.

Simpson, C.W. and Prusak, L. 'Troubles with Information Overload – moving from quantity to quality in information provision.' *International Journal of Information Management* 15(6), 1995, pp. 413-425.

Streufert, S.C. 'Effects of Information Relevance on Decision-making in Complex Environments.' *Memory and Cognition* 1, 1973, pp. 224-228.

Taylor, R. 'Age and Experience as Determinants of Managerial Information Processing and Decision-making Performance.' *Academy of Management Journal* 18, 1975, pp. 74-81.

Zmud, R. 'An Empirical Investigation of the Dimensionality of the Concept of Information.' *Decision Sciences* 9, 1978, pp. 187-195.

Chapter 6

Managers and information – the future

CHANGES IN THE INTERNAL AND EXTERNAL ENVIRONMENT

The previous chapters have concentrated on the use which managers make of information, the problems they encounter in locating it and their preferred sources of information. In this final chapter consideration is given to the effect that expected changes in the nature of what constitutes the manager's role and tasks will have on his/her requirements for information and how this information might be provided in the future. As Koch and Godden (1996) point out, there are likely to be fewer managers in organisations in the future, for a number of reasons:

- Cost-cutting – Koch and Godden (1996) point out that management is expensive and they suggest that in many organisations managers do not add much value to the product. They suggest that in a highly competitive environment organisations will not be able to sustain any overheads which are unproductive and consequently there will be a reduction in the number of traditional management posts in many organisations.

- Flattening of hierarchies within organisations – in many organisations the traditional tall organisational structure has been replaced by a much flatter hierarchy, often consisting of as few as three layers between those involved in 'shop-floor' activities and those involved in top management. This has been caused by several factors, two of which are particularly important:

  - movement towards a method of work which requires more self-managed teams in many areas of the organisation; consequently many of the decisions are taken by the team itself rather than requiring a decision to be passed up to a manager.

  - the move towards greater organisational democracy – as organisations become more knowledge-based, the workers, themselves, are likely to be more skilled and knowledgeable and less willing to be formally managed. They will require a greater say in what happens and if this is refused they are likely to move to somewhere where they believe that their views are regarded more seriously.

- Business process re-engineering – in organisations which have undergone business process re-engineering there are likely to be fewer functions which need to be managed, as well as a concentration on a more process-oriented way of doing things.

- Technology – the use of technology has reduced the need for individual collection of data which often formed a considerable part of the work of middle management. Koch and Godden (1996) point out that technology will be able to perform many of the control and operational tasks previously believed to fall to the manager.

These internal changes are also likely to be accompanied (and often accelerated) by changes in the external environment as more companies move from a national to a global perspective. Information and communication technologies will enable companies to compete in markets which were previously beyond their reach, but they will also find that competition in their own domestic markets is fiercer as other organisations use technology to extend their own competitive reach. The likely result of this is that as competition increases, the need to innovate will be greater and companies must respond positively to these challenges if they are to survive. It seems inevitable, therefore, that this shift in the business environment must be accompanied by changes both in the way in which managers define their role and in how they perform their tasks; this, in turn, is likely to be accompanied by changes in the type of information which managers seek and use and the manner in which it is delivered.

MANAGING IN THE FUTURE

Inevitably, as the pace of competition increases, many organisations will respond by making changes in many of the aspects of their business, including production, sales and distribution. As organisations become more knowledge-based and even make the transition to a learning organisation, the role of the manager will change from that of director and organiser to that of leader and team-coach; the manager will need to exert a less hands-on approach. The increasing use of the information and communication technologies and the rise of the knowledge-based organisation also seems likely to lead to an increase in teleworking and this will require a change in traditional methods of staff management.

Again, in the future the manager will not be required to spend so much time in data collection and control tasks as technology will carry out many of these tasks, but the continuing need for improvement in order to maintain market share, let alone increase it, seems likely to result in more managerial time spent with clients, customers and other stakeholders.

As globalisation and competition increases the complexity of the external environment, the need for a clear, well-planned strategy for the future of the organisation will become paramount. While information and communication technologies will enable a much greater competitive reach there will be few companies which can offer their products and services in every country in the world, so the management of the organisation will need to decide which areas of the world they wish to enter and which are the most appropriate into which to expand their current and future activities. Similarly, a more global presence will mean that there is a greater possibility of substitution of the organisation's products for those of others, constraints on trade will differ across boundaries and exchange rates and other commercial costs will fluctuate. In short, there will be a larger number of variables which need to be considered during the strategic planning process in the future and it seems likely, therefore, that the planning tasks will assume a greater amount of management time.

This increase in the number of variables which need to be considered will inevitably increase the amount of information which is required during the strategic planning task. As was demonstrated above, managers show a marked preference for personal verbal sources of information, believing that personal sources are likely to be more reliable and prefer the opportunities for feedback which the verbal sources provide. However, while current personal contacts are likely to be able to provide a valuable perspective on their own environment – the opportunities, competition, likely new entrants – they are less likely to be able to provide insights and information on new markets and opportunities in other parts of the world. Clearly, when a decision is made to enter a new market (or markets), personal contacts will be made and information collected from the members of this new network but, prior to making that decision, information will be required about which markets might be appropriate and which problems might be encountered. Information about possible opportunities, availability of incentives, and competition likely to be encountered will also be sought as well as much other background information. Such information will be extensive, often subjective, and frequently ambiguous and, as such, will require fairly careful analysis. Furthermore, it is likely to be in written form and, as was demonstrated above, managers dislike using written sources of information. Similarly, such information may well be available through the formally constituted information units within their own organisations which, as has been shown above, managers regard with suspicion. Somehow, however, this potentially relevant information must be provided to managers and they, in turn, must believe that they can rely on (and use) the information provided; there appear to be three choices:

- provide managers with access to all the available information services – both internal and external,

- provide a responsive information service staffed by people in whom the manager has confidence,

- a combination of these solutions.

Some managers, particularly those who have in the past complained about the problem of aggregated data from information systems, will prefer their own access to external and internal information systems. There is, however, a major problem with this solution: providing access does not necessarily imply effective use – the number of information databases and other sources of information is vast and many are widely available, so relevant, good quality information may be difficult to locate. Indeed, so great is the amount of potentially useful available information that its location and manipulation in a usable format might well occupy much of the manager's working day if he/she allowed it to do so. As was demonstrated above, however, managers are reluctant to spend a lot of time searching for and manipulating information because in doing so they are forced to neglect other tasks. The inevitable result of this choice, however, is likely to be the acquisition of less than adequate information which will have inevitable consequences for the future of the organisation. The obvious solution would seem to be that managers should pass the responsibility for the acquisition of information to others who not only have more time but are also trained for the task – for instance, the members of the organisation's formally constituted information unit. Given the lack of confidence discovered by many writers in information provided by such staff, however, it seems likely that few would be prepared to rely totally on the information provided by such people. It would seem that another solution to the problem of information provision to managers must be found which takes into account the research which has been done on how managers use information and which is, therefore, likely to increase the use of information by them.

As was demonstrated above, research shows that ease of access to information is of prime importance to managers and, while not guaranteeing the *use* of the information retrieved, providing simple access seems likely to increase the likelihood of information being used. It would seem sensible, therefore, to provide each manager with *easy access to quality sources* of information. Clearly, what constitutes a quality source for each manager would need to be investigated. For some managers a quality source might be a subscription to a commercially available information system or an account with a specialist provider of information services such as an information broker, for others a subscription to a service offering intelligent agent searching according to the manager's particular information profile will provide the solution. Similarly, the requirement for ease of access to such sources might imply the need for a direct line to such sources so the need for tedious logon procedures is avoided. This provision of easy access to quality information should enable the manager to provide confidently for many of his/her own information needs. However, the sheer variety of information services available and, indeed, the variety of information which the manager may require to satisfy the requirements of the global strategic planning exercise are likely to result in a requirement for additional assistance if much of the potentially relevant information is to be retrieved; this implies a need for people specialised in information sources. As we have seen, however, many managers have considerable reservations about the abilities of such people and are reluctant to use formally constituted information units within the organisation for several reasons:

- they perceive that the staff of such units lack any understanding of business,

- they do not regard the staff of such units as colleagues and so they are reluctant to rely on their opinion,

- the members of the unit are often perceived as loyal to the person to whom the unit reports rather than as providing a service to the organisation as a whole.

To provide for the information needs of managers, however, need not necessarily imply a requirement for a formally constituted information department within the organisation. It is not necessary that an organisation's information professionals should be collected together in a space formally designated as the information unit. Indeed, it seems probable that in future, many such units are likely to be virtual rather then actual physical units – there will be no floor space allocated to the information unit and those who work in the virtual unit may be teleworking, often at a considerable distance from the organisation – and perhaps providing services to the global organisation in the same manner as many other members of the organisation. Consequently, there is no good reason why the current formalised structure of the information unit should continue. Perhaps a better way to provide for the manager's needs would be to dispense with the formal information unit and allocate information workers to work as part of a particular manager's team rather than as part of the information unit team. Each manager would then be responsible for the recruitment of his/her information worker(s) and each such worker would play a part in the work of the team and share in its success, as well as being a cost as any other team member would be. This solution to the provision of information to management has much to recommend it; it would eliminate the problems of the information worker not being regarded as a colleague and also the problem of suspicions of their loyalty, and the manager and other team members would decide how relevant a knowledge of business might be to the success of the team and recruit accordingly. This solution addresses most of the major criticisms levelled against formally constituted information units and, in addition, it would also enable the information worker to provide a more customised service to the other members of the team because he/she would have a better knowledge of why information was required as well as what was wanted. Similarly, as the information worker would be working with other team members regularly he/she would develop an understanding of how they worked, their preferred modes of information structuring and formatting and so he/she would be able to improve the service offered to the members of the team. The brief of the information worker might be further extended; other tasks might include:

- to ensure that the information sources used by other team members are of high quality and are easily accessible;

- training of other team members on how to use the systems, how to access the information and manipulate and disseminate the information effectively and efficiently;

- maintenance of a 'watching brief' to ensure that the team uses the most appropriate, cost-effective and efficient sources of information and methods of mediation;

- management of the team's information, for instance provision of information on the team's network and ensuring that the team complies with the legal and organisational requirements for the collection and storage of information.

It seems probable that the manner in which the information team-worker provides information to the team might also need to change. Instead of the provision of hardcopy reports and online searches the information worker might be required to add value to the information by improved editing and more analysis. Similarly, dissemination of information to the team is likely to be mainly electronic but may also take the form of verbal team-briefings, thus acknowledging the preference for the verbal rather than the written word.

The provision of information to satisfy the many and varied needs of its managers is likely to prove a difficult exercise for many organisations, yet the correct mix of access to appropriate sources for personal managerial use coupled with the availability of personnel able to provide back-up services will be essential if appropriate information is to be made available to the organisation. It is this appropriate information which will inform the decision-making process which in turn will determine the success or otherwise of the organisation.

BIBLIOGRAPHY

Abell, Angela. 'Information Use and Business Success: a review of recent research of effective information delivery,' in *The Value and Impact of Information*, edited by Mary Feeney and Maureen Grieves (East Grinstead: Bowker-Saur, 1994).

Daft, Richard L. and Lengel, Robert H. 'Information Richness: a new approach to managerial behaviour and organisational design.' *Research in Organisational Behaviour* 6, 1984, pp. 191-233.

Daft, Richard L. and Lengel, Robert H. 'Organisational Information Requirements, media richness and structural design.' *Management Science* 32, 1986, pp. 554-571.

Daft, Richard L. Lengel, Robert H. and Trevino, Linda Klebe. 'Message Equivocality, Media Selection, and Manager Performance: implications for information systems.' *MIS Quarterly*, September 1987, pp. 355-366.

Drucker, Peter. 'The Coming of the New Organisation.' *Harvard Business Review* 1, 1988, pp. 45-53

Hammer, Michael and Champy, James. *Re-engineering the Corporation: a manifesto for business revolution* (London: Nicholas Brealey, 1993).

Handy, C. *The Age of Unreason* (London: Business Books, 1989).

KPMG Peat Marwick Management Consultants. *Information for Strategic Management: a survey of leading companies* (London: KPMG Peat Marwick Management Consultants, 1990).

Koch, Richard and Godden, Ian. *Managing Without Management: a post-management manifesto for business simplicity* (London: Nicholas Brealey, 1996).

Mintzberg, Henry. *The Nature of Managerial Work* (New York: Harper and Row, 1973).

Porter, M. *Competitive Strategy: techniques for analyzing industries and competitors* (New York: Free Press, 1980).

Porter, M. *Competitive Advantage: creating and sustaining superior performance* (New York: Free Press, 1985).

Porter M. and Miller, V. 'How Information Gives you a Competitive Advantage.' *Harvard Business Review,* July/August 1985, pp. 149-160.

Reuters Business Research. *To Know or Not to Know: the politics of information* (London: Reuters, 1994).

Reuters Business Research. *Dying for Information* (London: Reuters, 1996).

Senge, Peter. *The Fifth Discipline* (London: Century Business, 1990).

Stewart, Thomas A. *Intellectual Capital: the new wealth of nations* (London: Nicholas Brealey publishing, 1997).